T0268119

"Enjoyed it all the way... [Railey] *really caught the aura of the place."*

—*bestselling true crime writer* JERRY BLEDSOE,
author of Bitter Blood *and other works*

The
LOST COLONY
MURDER
on the
OUTER BANKS

SEEKING JUSTICE
FOR BRENDA JOYCE HOLLAND

JOHN RAILEY

THE
History
PRESS

Published by The History Press
Charleston, SC
www.historypress.com

Cover: Bridge photo by Aycock Brown, courtesy Outer Banks History Center, State Archives of North Carolina.

First published 2021

Manufactured in the United States

ISBN 9781467147392

Library of Congress Control Number: 2021931239

Notice: The information in this book is true and complete to the best of our knowledge. It is offered without guarantee on the part of the author or The History Press. The author and The History Press disclaim all liability in connection with the use of this book.

For Brenda

and for Kathleen

Contents

Contents

Acknowledgements

My thanks to all the sources, named and anonymous, who helped me bring this book together. The inside story of Brenda's case had never been told. It was buried for more than half a century. I heard from several Manteo residents who thought it should stay there. Fortunately, some islanders disagreed. They bravely came forward, both on the record and anonymously, generous with their time in my repeated phone calls, e-mails, private Facebook messages and visits.

Brenda's siblings—Ann Holland Earley, Charles Hoyt Holland and Kim Holland Thorn—bravely dug into long-suppressed pain to talk about their sister in the hopes of justice for her. Claudia Fry Sluder Harrington, the daughter of Dotty Fry and the former stepdaughter of Dr. Linus Edwards, and Buddy Tillett, who'd reopened the case while working as a deputy for the sheriff's office in 1995, proved invaluable in telling the story. Claudia generously shared her family's rich genealogical research. She provided solid editing as well.

The Outer Banks History Center in Manteo, led by Samantha Crisp and supported by North Carolina tax dollars and local donations, was a treasure-trove. Stuart Parks and Tama Creef of the center always answered my queries for photos and articles and promptly gave me fresh ideas on how to find more information.

The following people also helped greatly: Molly Griggs Miller, former Dare County deputy Sammy Smith, Jack Cahoon, Penny Twiford

Craven, Debbie Twiford Mueller, David Miller, Margaret Harvey, Quentin Bell, Della Basnight, Marilyn Whittington, Harriet Oneto, Dorothy Hester, Lisa Griggs, Carroll Leggett, Joseph L.S. Terrell, Al Matthews, Roy Riddick, former Manteo town manager Kermit Skinner, attorneys Mark and Vince Rabil, Earl Mirus, Dr. John Butts, Dr. Richard Sadler, cold-case SBI investigator Tony Cummings, SBI spokeswoman Paula McQuillan, Dare County sheriff Doug Doughtie, the family of Danny Barber, Paul Midgett, Mary Ann Edwards, Gladys Johnson, Nellie Heffron, Dottie Lowery, Lucien Morrissette, Marlene Cole, Maria Karnitschnig, former SBI agents W.A. "Doc" Hoggard and Jim Bailey, Chris Nunemaker, Drew Wilson, Robert Long, Amy Gaw, Beth Ownley Cooper, Jean Lipham Oates, Harry Niser Jr., Angel Ellis Khoury, Tony Duvall, Debra Johnson, Chip Py, McMullan Pruden, Cam Choiniere, acquisitions editor Kate Jenkins and senior editor Ryan Finn at The History Press, Bob Thorn, Snow Photo & Digital Imaging, lebame houston and Joseph L.S. Terrell.

My lifelong friend Blades Robinson, whose business is training for underwater investigations, took on Brenda's case as if it were his, enriching the book with his insights and his contacts. We both grew up hearing about the case as boys at Nags Head. My friend Drew Patton gave me insights for the book on a beach walk at Oak Island, a headquarters of our beloved McClellan clan.

Tony Clark, the former publisher of the *Coastland Times*; the paper's general manager, Theresa Schneider; and former managing editor Kari Pugh encouraged me, generously edited and ran my columns on the case and relayed tips on it to me. Seth Effron at WRAL-TV in Raleigh picked up the columns, as did John Drescher, then at the *News & Observer* of Raleigh, generating more tips. Reporter Rachael Cardin, then at WTKR in Norfolk, covered our fight well. Legendary Outer Banks photographer Aycock Brown is long gone, but his classic photos, including one used on the cover of this book, gave me the dreamscape to bring characters alive.

My favorite Nags Head bar, Sam & Omie's, run by my friend Carole Sykes, provided me with just the spot to find inside sources. My friends Jerry Bledsoe and Mary Giunca gave the manuscript a careful read and supplied many suggestions to make it better.

My "Uncle Billy" Tarkington of Manteo and the Ocean House motel in Kill Devil Hills first told me Brenda's story. He and his venerable motel are long gone, but his storytelling lives. Ditto for the stories my fellow workers at the Seafare restaurant in Nags Head weaved.

My late parents, Hazel and Dick Railey, taught me to love the beach and fight injustice, starting in their turquoise dream of a cottage by the ocean in Nags Head with my siblings Richard, Jo and Mimi. My daughter, Molly Fincher, and her husband and children share that love of the beach and keep me laughing.

Most of all, thanks to my bride, Kathleen, who never gives up on me as she tirelessly helps me turn my dreams into books. Into the mystic, my love.

Author's Note

I think one thing that attracts us to islands is the sense of belonging their residents have. That is what drew me to this story as a child and keeps me there now. I spent much of my formative years in Nags Head and often ventured to nearby Manteo. I envy the tight bonds and loyalty the Roanoke Islanders share. They are loath to tell their secrets.

This is a story about an outsider, Brenda Joyce Holland, who was killed on Roanoke Island in the summer of 1967. The suspects in her slaying—some of whom were outsiders, some of whom were islanders—were each confronting what it means to belong or to be cast out.

Much of this story is about flawed lawmen. I am indebted to the families of some of those men, who let me in and candidly shared their loved ones' stories. Redemption rings for these men who find their footing later in the story.

In this, the first nonfiction book on Brenda's unsolved case, I have relied on unique access to the sealed SBI file, hundreds of interviews with her siblings, case insiders and other islanders telling their stories for the first time, newspaper articles and a thick file on Brenda that her sister Kim compiled.

Most of the dialogue in this book comes verbatim from those documents and interviews. Other dialogue has been re-created based on those sources. The names Rob Breeze, Molly Black, Jay Fieldman, Coy Dupree and Houston Rob Waters are pseudonyms to protect privacy. All other names are real. The names of Manteo streets are those used in 1967, instead of names that were changed in the years afterward. Several people in this story share the Midgette and Midgett surnames. None of them are directly related, although it's said on the Outer Banks that all the Midgette families are distantly related, tied through their proud history.

JOHN RAILEY
Nags Head, North Carolina
October 2020

*"Personally, I doubt there is anything to know. Things happen.
Good things, bad things, things no one understands. They happen."
Makepeace shrugged. "Life goes on."*

—*Caicos Island commissioner Birds Makepeace responding to an outsider's
question about a local mystery in Peter Benchley's 1979 novel* The Island

*Now down the trackless, hollow years
That swallowed them, but not their song,
We send response…*

—*from the opening lines of Paul Green's* The Lost Colony

THE CAST

THE VICTIM
Brenda Joyce Holland

THE INVESTIGATORS
Dare County sheriff Frank Cahoon
State Bureau of Investigation agents Lenny Wise, Dan Gilbert,
       Jack Thomas, Charlie Ray and Clyde Fentress
Manteo police chief C.C. Duvall, who became one of Sheriff Cahoon's
       top deputies
Duvall's successor, Manteo police chief Ken Whittington Sr.
Dare County deputy R.D. "Buddy" Tillett

THE PHOTOGRAPHER
Aycock Brown, head of the Dare County Tourist Bureau and
       shooter for *The Lost Colony* and the *Coastland Times*

THE PRIME SUSPECTS
Danny Barber
Rodney Brett
John Langston Daniels
Dr. Linus Matthew Edwards
John Davis Scarborough
David Edward Whaley

The Cast

BRENDA'S FAMILY
Parents Charles "Shotgun" Holland and Gerri Holland
Siblings Ann Holland Earley, Charles Hoyt Holland and
        Kim Holland Thorn

PROLOGUE

I t's the summer of 2018, but it might as well be half a century before as the man is asked about the nineteen-year-old woman found dead in the sound in July 1967. Brenda Joyce Holland's body, bloated past her beauty, was zipped up in a black bag and placed in a black hearse that drove her to a cold autopsy slab in Norfolk, Virginia, a city she never saw in life.

This man knows things. A lot of things. And he just might talk. He hints, "You have to remember: In Manteo, there are no secrets." Brenda's case has been reopened. Nobody wants to talk about it to outsiders. But Manteo never forgets.

My host is cordial, offering iced water as he vapes. He is the ultimate local, and he is a private sort. But after I find my way through a byzantine maze to our meeting spot, he receives me warmly and agrees to talk as long as his name is not used. He is impish and by turns wry and emotional as he describes a mystery man, a suspect in the case who sang in a choir like an angel.

Near our meeting spot is Shallowbag, the yacht-splashed bay that elbows around downtown Manteo. Hundreds of tourists are walking the sun-kissed streets, revitalized to the point it's sort of a cosmic blend of a New England seafaring town and a sanitized Key West. Manteo is the seat of Dare County, which takes in eighty miles of dreamy beaches, but Manteo, near the center of Roanoke Island, is very much its own deal—always has been. It's the larger of the two villages on the island, a spot of sand between mainland Dare and the Outer Banks beaches, surrounded by sounds and anchored by pines, live oaks, yaupons, marshlands and its own sense of right and wrong. On the south end of the island is Wanchese, a commercial fishing bedrock and home to some of the roughest, toughest fighters in the world—whether they're hauling in catches afar in high seas in treacherous spots such as the Grand Banks off Newfoundland or just holding their own in local bars.

Manteo is just as hard. It's just quieter about it. Maybe that difference goes back to the namesakes of the two places: Manteo, the Croatan Indian who worked with those colonists who would become famously lost off his island, and Wanchese, his fellow Indian who always had a healthy dose of skepticism about the English.

The villages named for those Indians, separated by fewer than five miles, share bloodlines if not sensibilities. But Manteo has always had its share of brutality, bruising fights in beat-down bars like Nick's House of Joy bar in "California," one of the Black sections of town, or in the modest white neighborhoods surrounding it. There was also hard partying and occasional brutality in the well-to-do area, Mother Vineyard, at least in one house on the Roanoke Sound, where local children often played with the children of Andy Griffith, who lived nearby. The Mother Vineyard area is named for a scuppernong grapevine, several hundred years old and counting, that is believed to be the oldest cultivated grapevine in the United States. It may date back to the time of the first English colonists in 1585, even before the lost colony.

There has always been a magic and meanness to Manteo.

Brenda Holland, who'd just completed her sophomore year at Campbell College in Buies Creek, North Carolina, got the magic in the summer of 1967. It was her first time in Manteo. As the nineteen-year-old makeup supervisor at *The Lost Colony*, the nighttime outdoor drama on the island, Brenda reveled in the company made up of locals and artists from around the country. She and many of the rest, boarding in local houses, would hit the normally quiet streets of Manteo after work. The town was theirs for the summer.

My host remembers how cool was the sound of their laugher, riding the soft salt breezes of the coastal night, drifting into his window, open in the manner of the time on the island. He was fifteen that summer of 1967. "I didn't know what all they were doing," he says, "but I couldn't wait to be part of it."

Then he tells me about that suspect who sang like an angel in *The Lost Colony* choir: "This is kind of emotional for me. Danny Barber taught me to waterski." He nods at my wide eyes. Danny Barber, Brenda's date on the night she vanished, is a key suspect in the case—the main suspect for some people. He went back to college the summer after her slaying and was said to have never returned to the island. His absence ramped up a widespread belief that he'd killed Brenda.

There is an iconic news photo of him from the day Brenda's body was found. Barber has been summoned to her hearse by Dare County sheriff Frank Cahoon to identify her. The suspect wears a crew-neck, blue-and-white-striped shirt tucked neatly into belted blue jeans. His brown hair is short, and his beard is neatly

Brenda Joyce Holland in one of her publicity shots for *The Lost Colony. Courtesy Kim Holland Thorn.*

trimmed. It's a close-up shot, or at least an attempted one, but Barber's head is turned to the right, his eyes masked by the angle and the glasses he wears. His buff arms are crossed at his waist.

I mention that Barber was a fit guy. My host settles back in his seat, crosses his legs and smiles sadly. "Yeah," he says, "he was burly. But he was nice. And gentle."

My host's family, like so many in Manteo, had a motorboat. He used it to take members of the *Lost Colony* company waterskiing. That's how he met Barber. "God, could he ski," my host says. Soon Barber was giving him one-on-one lessons, teaching him how to slalom, to dance across the water.

We talk of other main suspects, including a dentist and a troubled party boy who was the grandson of the local Episcopal priest. We talk about an African American suspect from Manteo who was informed on by his white lover.

Our chat winds back to Barber. On a morning shortly after Brenda vanished, my host met him at the downtown dock for his skiing lesson. Barber showed up on time, but he told him he couldn't give him his lesson. My host never got to talk to him again. Barber stayed in town for the rest of *The Lost Colony* season, but he was withdrawn as State Bureau of Investigation agents, in the audience every night, kept watch on him.

My host keeps talking, re-creating the island town of more than a half century past and conveying the pulse of Manteo today. The times merge.

Brenda Holland is out there still, calling to us from her last hours, the darkness before dawn on the first day of July 1967. Then as now on Outer Banks nights, car headlights flash on girls and young women walking by the road. In some of those passing cars, local folks of long memory worry that those girls will not make it home. They think of Brenda.

In the summer of 1967, the mystery of what happened to her went nationwide. Reporters in fedoras descended on the island. It was the biggest story in North Carolina, with each new revelation from investigators making front-page headlines in the newspapers, alongside stories of race riots in the big cities nationwide and President Johnson mired in the Vietnam War. Mothers on the beaches near Manteo hugged their babies all the tighter. Children shivered as their parents told them what they knew of Brenda's story, pointing to her photo in the 1967 *Lost Colony* program and then turning the pages to a photo of Barber, saying he was the killer.

The parents and reporters didn't know a fraction of the real story, which investigators closely guarded. The civilians didn't know about all the turns the case would take, some almost mystical, ranging from an apparent shallow grave to a candlelight séance to a surprise found hiding in a "coffin." They didn't know about the mentally challenged local man, the town's unofficial "night watchman," being targeted by a Manteo lawman.

There was homophobia and racism as North Carolinians from afar urged investigators to check out "well-known homosexuals" or certain "colored people." The locals, as always, wanted to know all they could about their fellow residents, whom they usually did not judge. But during that summer of 1967, the investigation infected Manteo. In a small town on a small island, family snitched on family and lovers on lovers. Neighbors informed on neighbors in clandestine, fear-filled meetings with investigators, and employers informed on employees.

It was a summer so awash in booze that those grilled by investigators were all over the place about times and stories. "You have to remember," an islander would say years later, "everybody drank."

But not the victim—well, at least, not hardly. All these years later, Brenda, who'd let a can of beer go hot before finishing it, jumps out at us still. In Manteo today, you can still talk to people who knew and loved her—that woman who descended from the cloud-splitting Smoky Mountains. Brenda rode into Manteo in her handmade but stylish clothes at the dawn of the

Summer of Love, her mod colors and designs fitting with the mood of the company she joined. Even her black-and-white photo from *The Lost Colony* program captures her big eyes and welcoming smile. She spent just one month in Manteo, but her name will forever be linked with the town. One of the best months of her life, June 1967, ended, and her body was found floating in the Albemarle Sound as July began. She'd been strangled and, quite possibly, raped.

She was buried back up in the mountains on the day after what should have been her twentieth birthday. A rain shower ended as they lowered her flower-draped white casket into her family plot in a valley just up the road from her homeplace.

She did not like rain, but she came to love the ocean and wrote letters home of beach bonfires. She loved the way the sea bleached and transformed ordinary pieces of wood into strange and wonderful things—some that looked like beasts bounding on the beach, others like foreign animals at rest. She loved feeling the sand on her bare feet, watching dolphins play and staring out at the limitless sea, ever-changing, from happy green to mean gray and all shades in between. She loved the way the morning mist rose off the sounds like ghosts in a place where the present and past blended, where locals still spoke in an Old English brogue. Tide was "toide" and ice was "oice." She loved the way sea breezes carried conversations, how you could stand on the beach and hear fragments of chats from fifty yards away.

She poured her imagination into a play that ends with the question of what happened to the lost colony in the late 1500s. Andy Griffith got his start in *The Lost Colony* twenty years before playing a soldier, then graduating in subsequent seasons to playing Sir Walter Raleigh (an "Englishman with a Southern accent," as Griffith once put it). He fell in love with Manteo. After the weekend performances of the pageant, Griffith the comedian would go on stage at a local club, testing his *Hamlet* monologue, a country boy's interpretation of Shakespeare that would become a classic. He made it in the TV production of *No Time for Sergeants* and later in the Broadway play and film version by the same name. Soon thereafter, he landed his namesake show on TV, playing the sheriff in a small town called "Mayberry," and had a soundfront house in Manteo. He was often seen around barefoot, hanging out with the islanders.

Observers from afar said that Mayberry was a fictional version of Griffith's hometown of Mount Airy, Andy's North Carolina hometown. But he would later say, "If Mayberry is anywhere, it is Manteo," Angel Ellis Khoury writes in *Manteo: A Roanoke Island Town*.

Brenda's parents during World War II, Charles "Shotgun" Holland and Geraldine "Gerri" Holland. *Courtesy Charles Hoyt Holland.*

Brenda stared wide-eyed at Griffith that summer, when his show was a major prime-time event. Brenda being Brenda, she might have glided up to him and asked for career connections and an autograph—not for her, of course, but for her little brother and sister. She would have told herself that, anyway.

And then Brenda and her summer were gone. Key suspects went back to college. Others remained on the island. For the general public, the terror visited on Brenda faded as the newspaper clippings about her case yellowed. There are hundreds of thousands of stories about the lost colonists and hundreds of books about them, but little is penned about Brenda.

She floats alone in that summer of 1967. The trauma of what happened to her never ebbed for her parents, Gerri and Charles Wiley "Shotgun" Holland. Four centuries before, John White, the governor of the Roanoke Colony, may never have gotten over the mystery of what happened to his daughter Eleanor Dare, his granddaughter Virginia and the rest of the lost colonists. It was personal for him, just as the mystery of what happened to their daughter Brenda was for her parents, gnawing at them all their days. The pain of losing a daughter transcends centuries. Just as Virginia Dare is locked away in memories of her as an infant, Brenda is locked in memories of her at nineteen. That trauma continues to this day for Brenda's siblings. And it continues for someone else, a woman who was tied as a child to one of the suspects. She and Brenda's siblings are bound in pain if not in blood.

Part I

THE TOWN AND THE CRIME

MANTEO, NORTH CAROLINA
JUNE AND JULY 1967

Soaring

Dear Folks,

At this moment I'm looking down at the city of Fayetteville. There are millions of little lights—all colors—and then there's darkness. There are fewer lights now and I can see few lights at all....We're awfully high up now—everything is so hazy—kinda peaceful-like.

Love,
"B"

—Brenda Joyce Holland in a letter to her parents about her first flight, a January 25, 1967 trip to Washington, D.C.

Around 9:00 a.m. on the last day of May 1967, Darrell Midgette pulled his black Ford sedan up in front of the Spainhour boardinghouse where Brenda Holland lived in Buies Creek, North Carolina, and honked his horn. It was a town of a few hundred souls anchored by Campbell College, the school Darrell and Brenda attended. Up in her room, Brenda probably gave one last glimpse in the mirror. She would have seen big brown eyes and a warm smile, a face filled with openness. She wasn't perfect: there was a slight gap between her front teeth. That made her all the more attractive. She was five feet, seven inches tall and 120 pounds—long legs and model looks with a nineteen-inch waist.

Brenda at Campbell College. *Courtesy Kim Holland Thorn.*

She would have given *the hair* one last pat—*the hair* that was newly cut short into a bob and dyed. Not even three weeks before, on Friday, May 12, Brenda had written on her calendar in her bubbly cursive, "Became a blond!" Brenda of the brown locks no more. Her mom wouldn't approve, but her mother frosted her own brown hair, even if she didn't wear it in a modern bob.

Brenda was headed to the Outer Banks, to Manteo, to work as the makeup supervisor for *The Lost Colony* outdoor drama on Roanoke Island. She was active in her college's theater community and dreamed of making a career in the field. She had studied the profession and the paths to success, including going to New York and waiting tables and other odd jobs while making connections. Brenda charted a more cautious path, realizing that her parents would never approve of her setting out for the Big Apple. She had to overcome her mother's objections just to get to college. She was the first person in her family to go, having just completed her sophomore year at Campbell, a small Baptist school about a forty-five-minute drive south of the state capital of Raleigh.

Brenda knew that *The Lost Colony* had Broadway and Hollywood connections among its former and current casts. She battled her parents over her decision to take the theater job at the far end of their state. Brenda was pushing the boundaries, soaring past the cloistered culture in which she was raised in the Western North Carolina mountains just outside Canton.

Darrell, a biology major from Manteo and fellow sophomore she occasionally dated, was driving her down to the coast since she didn't have a car. He was tall with brown hair, active in student government, serious in his studies but fun as well—the kind of guy who would do anything for his friends. He liked to sing and play his guitar, two of his favorites being the ballads "Harbor Lights" and "Smoke Gets in Your Eyes." He was steady, accustomed to Brenda's effervescence. If she was giggly and anxious, he was as placid as the water in the sounds of his region on a good day.

Protests for civil rights and against the Vietnam War were roiling campuses in other towns and cities. There was much talk of "the Establishment" world of parents versus the "the Anti-Establishment" world of their children. But not on the cozy Campbell campus.

For this summer anyway, *The Lost Colony* was calling Brenda away. She earned her job through her strong theater work at Campbell, which had close connections with the play. Paul Green, who wrote the play during the Great Depression, had grown up in Buies Creek. He embraced Roanoke Island, building on the enthusiasm the islanders had long had for telling their story and celebrating it.

Brenda had never been to an island. The closest she had come was watching *Gilligan's Island*, the primetime TV comedy about a group of shipwrecked castaways.

Brenda's parents hated the idea of her going to Manteo. They were mountain people, not coastal people. They'd never been to the Outer Banks. They wanted her to come back home that summer and resume her job at a local drive-in, where she could make more money. Her dad was protective of his middle daughter. Brenda kept working on her parents, just as she had when she moved off campus to live at Mrs. Spainhour's boardinghouse.

In a letter to her parents the previous January 26 about her first flight, a trip to Washington, D.C., she'd carefully dropped in her pitch for her off-campus move. She began the letter with "Dear Folks." Those folks were Charles Wiley Holland and Geraldine Ray "Gerri" Holland. Charles Holland was five feet, seven inches tall and, maybe, mountain-river wet, 165 pounds. But he was all fight, a man whose friends had nicknamed him "Shotgun" for his outrages. After he graduated from high school, he went to work in the Canton paper mill, like his father and many other relatives before him. When World War II broke out, he joined the army. He served in Europe, driving officers around because he'd learned to speak French and German in high school. He rose to sergeant. He had a lively and active mind. He saw combat, for which he won a Bronze star. He fought at the Battle of the Bulge. He was wiry and hard-drinking, tempered by his gentle bride, who had taken his name before he shipped out for the war. Over there, he savored the photos he'd taken of the petite and beautiful blue-eyed Gerri and punched out fellow servicemen who leered at those photos over his shoulder. In photos of him during the war, he comes across as darkly handsome and moody, like Montgomery Clift in *From Here to Eternity*, another story of World War II. Just as with Clift in the movie, Shotgun Holland was an underdog forever snarling from his chain.

Gerri was smart, too, but had to drop out of school in the seventh grade to look after her younger siblings. She later got her GED.

Shotgun came home when the war ended in 1945. He had seen his firstborn, Ann, just once, on leave, before he shipped out. She was three when he returned. He went back to work at the mill. Its sprawling buildings anchored the town and stood tall over it. Its stacks constantly belched exhaust into the Smoky Mountains, leaving in its wake the smothering smell of sulfur, like rotten eggs, that the locals had long since accepted as the smell of money. Work in the mill was tedious and hard. Shotgun Holland and his family and friends punched the timeclock. The paper mill was the only money game in town.

Shotgun worked his way up to floor supervisor and, with Gerri, raised, successively, Ann, Brenda, Charles Hoyt ("Little Charles") and the baby of the family, Kim. They lived in a brick house on Old Asheville Road in the shadow of Holland Mountain, which had been in Shotgun's family for generations. The war kept coming back to him, including memories of the blood-soaked snow of the Battle of the Bulge. He worked hard and played hard, retreating to his basement, where he planted himself in his father's rocking chair by a woodstove. There he drank his bourbon and beer, smoked his Kool cigarettes, watched TV and stoked his woodstove and anger. The news reports were all about the Vietnam War and the hippies protesting it, barely mentioning his war. There were situation comedies about his war, like *McHale's Navy*, about sailors in the South Pacific, and *Hogan's Heroes*, with American soldiers in a prisoner of war camp in Germany, but those shows were free of the brutality he saw. He turned the dial on his TV to western dramas. He knew they weren't realistic either. But they were not as insulting as the war comedies.

Sometimes when he was drunk, Shotgun would punish his children for what he saw as transgressions, ripping off his belt and whipping them. Brenda once ran to a relative's house after he whipped her. Gerri and Shotgun argued about his drinking. They fought about money. Gerri liked nice things. For a while, she had this big car. "When you have a Cadillac," she said, "people just notice you."

Shotgun would slap, push and shove Gerri in front of their children. The scenes haunted Brenda. Gerri would flee with the children, going to a relative's house and returning after a few days. Wherever his war memories might take him, Shotgun Holland's children were his life. He would kill for them.

The Hollands were not wealthy, but they had land. Shotgun Holland, wearing his fatigue jacket from the war, would lead his children through briars to the top of their mountain, to a place where their ancestors had lived in a log cabin that still stood. Near high cliffs, Shotgun would tell his children about the Indians buried up there in the clouds, the wolves that once roamed and how one of his ancestors had killed a man on the mountain trail in an argument over a woman. He'd tell them about growing up on that mountain, about confronting rattlesnakes and reloading his twenty-gauge double-barrel just in time to blow them away. Ever after, he would tell them, he could sense the musky odor of those things with no shoulders.

Brenda was lively and dramatic, all pigtails and beaming eyes. Her elementary school teachers praised her in report cards. "Thank you for letting me have your little girl to teach and love these last two years," Mrs. Cook, who taught her for first and second grades, wrote on Brenda's report card.

As she hit Canton High School, Brenda's family dynamic shifted. The oldest child, Ann, married. The baby of the family, Kim, was often sick with chronic asthma. Gerri, having lost her baby sister to asthma, was scared and doted on Kim. Brenda helped with both of her younger siblings. She became the daughter-in-charge.

Brenda took Little Charles on dates with her and showed up in church with little children clinging to her like ornaments on a Christmas tree, boys in bangs and girls in pigtails.

Ann Holland Earley with her little sister Brenda in the 1950s. *Courtesy Ann Holland Earley.*

Brenda at a high school dance.
Courtesy Kim Holland Thorn.

Brenda was a member of a musical group, the Highland Minstrels. In a sepia photo made during a session at a local radio station, she holds a bass guitar, standing by bandmates Freddie Ruth Plemmons on banjo and Jean Lipham on mandolin. The photo verges on campy, but Brenda is no hillbilly. Her hair is brown, long and straight until it cascades across her lean shoulders, where it flips up gently, a carefree look achieved by painstaking effort with hot curlers. It's the warm eyes and gentle smile that get you. She's open and honest, pretty but not stuck-up. Jean Lipham, from the band, was Brenda's best friend. Brenda was always encouraging her, telling her to "Chin up, buckaroo."

Brenda confided in girls and in boys, and they in her. When she was a junior in high school, she corresponded with a man from Canton who'd become a marine. In a May 12, 1963 letter from Camp Lejeune, North Carolina, he told her "the real story" about an acquaintance of theirs who'd gone AWOL in that mindstorm of a time with death and maiming in Vietnam looming:

> *He said in a joking tone, "Doyle, let's go over the hill tonight. I honestly thought he was joking....Then the next day, he asked me if I would leave with him that night, and I told him I wasn't leaving under no circumstances except an emergency....I tried to talk to him but I didn't have time to say as much as I should have, although I did try to explain to him what trouble it would bring.*

Canton family doctor Hugh Archie Matthews, who'd delivered Brenda on July 8, 1947, and was from Buies Creek, nudged her to attend Campbell. Shotgun liked the idea of Brenda going to college; Gerri Holland did not. She and her husband had both struggled to survive as children in the Great Depression. She worried that they didn't have enough money to send Brenda to college. She was envious of her daughter's close relationship with the Matthews family, and she didn't see the importance of college. She didn't want Brenda to be so far away from home. But Brenda was determined to

Brenda receiving her diploma from Canton High School. *Courtesy Kim Holland Thorn.*

go, to escape her small town and build a new life far away. Such ancient divides between parents and children had been tagged with a new name in the 1960s: "the Generation Gap."

Ultimately, Dr. Matthews helped Brenda with tuition and introduced her to his friends at Campbell. Brenda dug into the school's drama program, reveling in the hot swirl of backstage work. As the costumer for the Campbell Players, she applied her ingenuity and imagination to the backstage details of plays, including *Brigadoon* and *Oklahoma*. She worried that she wasn't earning her keep in her paid job as costumer. "I'm thinking about staying here during the semester break so I can do some necessary work for the drama department because I don't feel that I've done as much as I was paid for," she wrote to her mother on January 14, 1967.

Brenda became a master of the college backstage, singing along with one of the signature lines from *Oklahoma!*: "...where the wind comes sweeping down the plain!" The girl had her father's fire and her mom's ability to get along with people. And she had learned how to get what she wanted from her parents, as in that request to move off campus. She appealed to her mom in the January 26 letter:

> *Mom, I need you to write another letter to the dean of women....The reason—I am moving out of the dorm, I am going to stay with Mrs. W.W. Spainhour....Mrs. Spainhour is so nice, a widow, and lives right on the edge of campus. I wrote to the Tuition Plan to get a release for my room and found it will be $20 a month, much less than it was in the dorm. I hope you and Dad approve—I'll miss life in the dorm but I think I will be better off....I am still under all the rules that I was in the dorm. It's just that there will be a little less pressure—gosh, I hope you aren't mad at this "doing" before telling you. Let me try to explain—I've been contemplating this for a long time but haven't seen a chance to move out of the dorm to a private home so I just didn't talk about it.*

Brenda wrote that she'd already gotten approval from the appropriate college officials for her move. "So, now there it is. I had a specific time and I had to decide for myself. I do so hope you agree with me—Anyway, I need you to write your permission....All you need to say is that I may move in with Mrs. W.W. Spainhour. I would have called but I hated to run up the phone bill. This must get in before I get back to school. I have to move out by Wednesday."

Later in the letter, she wrote about her flight to Washington, riffing into light-hearted science fiction aimed at her little brother and sister:

> *My goodness—there's a flying saucer—there it is on the tip of our wing and there are Martians getting out—or are they Plutonians? They appear friendly enough. One of them is looking at me—they're darling little*

creatures in their gold spacesuits and red helmets and they're only about 12 inches tall. Oh, he's talking to me—he wants me to take a ride in his ship. I must go—I may never have this chance again.

It was a lovely ride. We zoomed all over America. It's a beautiful land, you know. If only it could have lasted longer. The little guy's name was Mercurton and he lives on the planet Venus. He was very intelligent and taught me the meaning of friendship. I was only with him for five earth minutes but it was a year in their time zone because he made it last that long. I will tell you sometime some of the things he taught me. I can now laugh at my problems.

As she wrote those words, America was at the height of its fascination with space and space heroes. On the day Brenda was born, the *Roswell Daily Press* of New Mexico headlined the "capture of a flying saucer." By the time U.S. military officials said it was merely the crash of an army air force weather balloon, the hype and hysteria that would boom for years to come had taken off. But the space fascination had a serious side as well. In May 1961, President Kennedy, as part of his New Frontier, announced his goal of putting a man on the moon by the end of the decade. By the mid-1960s, President Johnson, in his hokey manner, was pushing his slain predecessor's dream. Astronauts were almost as big as the Beatles. The TV shows *Star Trek* and *Lost in Space*—with its moralistic robot's iconic line of "Danger Will Robinson!"—were popular. In the science fiction TV shows of the 1960s, heroes always rushed in and saved the innocents, just as they did in the westerns Brenda's father loved.

Brenda was tuned into her culture as well as her country. In the letter, she gushed about Washington:

The view of D.C. from the air was beyond description. I could see the Capitol building, Washington Monument, etc., so clearly. We've gone sightseeing every day. Yesterday we walked up the Washington Monument—it's only about 40 stories, 555-feet high! I'll never try that again because I was about dead when we reached the top! I walked into the Lincoln Memorial also. Oh my, I've learned so much I can't begin to tell you all I've seen. I get the biggest thrill every time we cross the Potomac River by way of Arlington Memorial Bridge. In front of you is the Lincoln Memorial and behind is the Arlington Memorial Gateway. And the river is absolutely beautiful. Today we're going to the zoo, maybe. Tomorrow the Smithsonian.

Brenda's year had started off well. But there'd been some dips, including illness. In a January 14 letter to her mother, Brenda wrote:

> *Am having a fight with myself; I'm trying to get sick again. I have swollen glands and I am as nervous as a cat. But I made it up in my mind that I've got to take care of myself and not let myself get so bad I can't go to class. So I'm taking some medicine which they gave me the last time I was sick and I am dressing as warmly as I can. Mom, I also need that beige coat, I'm sorry. I'll buy one this summer because I need one so bad. Hey, don't worry about me trying to get sick, I'm going to be a big girl and take care of myself, O.K.?*

She ended the missive:

> *Well, I'll be closing for now. I'll try to write during the next two weeks but don't think I'm not thinking about you if I don't. I've got to where I don't even go to my mailbox. You…write so seldom and no one else writes to me so there is really no need to. Be sweet and take care of yourself.*
>
> *Love,*
> *Brenda*

The year got better as spring came on: the plays she loved working on, the friends she loved, the trips they took. In early May 1967, she went to Morehead City, on the North Carolina coast a few hours south of Manteo, for a literary retreat. Then back to Campbell for exams and the big move to the island. Her folks had to sign a contract for her to take the forty-five-dollar-per-week job with *The Lost Colony*. They did so, reluctantly. Another thing that bothered them: she hadn't been home since Easter, the last week of March, when she'd caught a ride home with a friend. Gerri Holland had gotten Brenda and the rest of her children to their church, Ridgeway Baptist, that Sunday. Shotgun and Gerri had raised their children at Ridgeway because it was a few miles from their brick home on Old Asheville Road. Recently, they'd purchased a family plot in the garden of stone on a hill by the church. One day, Shotgun and Gerri figured, Brenda and the rest of their children would lay them down there.

Just a few weeks after that Easter Sunday, Brenda called her parents to say she wouldn't have a chance to get home before leaving for her *Lost Colony* job. Her parents were not pleased. They worried about her, as always. Ann was only about four years older than Brenda, but she was calmer, married and living in Canton.

Brenda's little brother, Charles, got a bad vibe about her plans. He was twelve and worshiped her. She was always pushing him in school. He was just as smart as she was, she'd tell him, and he could get to college too. He hung on her words. But he worried about her going to Manteo.

As she left her room in Buies Creek that last day of May, Brenda took her 1967 calendar off the wall and rolled it into her suitcase along with a paperback, *Zorba the Greek*. She had marked on the calendar dates with boys, play rehearsals and exams. It was a Columbia Records calendar and noted on the bottom, "Music to live with. All Year Long." Album references on the bottom of the May page included Pete Seeger's *We Shall Overcome* and *Frank Sinatra's Greatest Hits*. Even Sinatra was struggling to keep up with the times. The summer before, when he was fifty, he'd married the actress Mia Farrow, who was twenty-one.

Brenda grabbed a treasured necklace off the top of the dresser and put it on. It was a thin silver chain with a small locket that delineated her as Miss Congeniality for Haywood County, 1966. Brenda won it at a beauty pageant back home the previous summer.

She hurried out of the Spainhours' house, giving a hug to Mrs. Spainhour and her roommate and Campbell classmate Pat Patrick. She and Brenda had spent hours sharing stories of their big and small dramas, talk of boys and ideas and future plans.

Brenda waltzed out to the quiet street. Darrell Midgette opened the trunk of his car. Brenda deposited her suitcase and her hanging bag of dresses. She settled into the bucket seat on the passenger side for the four-hour ride, sliding off her sandals to go barefoot, in the mood for the beach. Their ride began. They might have talked of school, of Darrell's ease with biology and Brenda's struggles with it. They probably talked about the intrigues and romances of their mutual friends. And Darrell surely began to fill Brenda in on his hometown, Manteo. He drove steadily northeast, soon getting onto U.S. 64 East, the long two-lane road to the coast.

On Darrell's push-button AM radio, they would have listened to the latest music. Out West, hippies converging in the Haight-Ashbury section of San Francisco were launching the Summer of Love. Earlier that month, the song telling hippies coming to San Francisco to "be sure to wear flowers" in their hair had been released. Dr. Timothy Leary was pushing LSD use, urging people to "turn on, tune in, drop out." Among some young people, LSD was better than God. Young women on birth control pills were feeling almost as free about sex as men.

Brenda was no hippie. Her clothes, most of which she made, were quietly stylish. She didn't do drugs and hardly drank—just a bit of beer now and then. She didn't sleep around, but she wasn't a "square" either. She liked boys and she liked to get out, to have all kinds of conversations with all kinds of folks.

By early afternoon, they would have been within an hour of Manteo. They passed through Columbia, on the chocolate-colored water of the Scuppernong River, with its quiet downtown, and then crossed the Alligator River on a drawbridge. They might have had a delay of fifteen minutes or so if the bridge-tender swung the bridge open for a tall-masted boat to come through. But such delays weren't that onerous—a chance to step out of the car, stretch and suck in the air.

A sign at the end of the bridge marked the Dare County line. That "Dare" name would have resonated with Brenda. The county formed in 1870 is named for Virginia Dare, the first child born of English parents in America, a milestone featured in the play Brenda was about to join. But maybe even more than that, the provocative nature of the word *dare* might have hit her. She was entering a place that had, since its inception, been all about taking dangerous chances. There was the colony that had vanished. The county was home to descendants of those who'd shipwrecked off its shores, as well as modern-day outcasts, adrift from families, responsibilities, big cities and other problems. Some people came to Dare to find themselves. Others came to lose themselves. It was a place of both forgiveness and foreboding.

As they entered the mainland portion of Dare County, they passed tarpaper shacks close to the road with patched clothes drying on lines and snarling dogs with flea-bitten hides clinging tight to their ribs. The highway soon cut through thick pine woods and swamps. They passed through the commercial fishing village of Manns Harbor. Leathery men in T-shirts were unloading the day's catch, cigarettes hanging from their chapped lips, the veins in their tattooed arms standing out and their sea-beaten boats bobbing in an oil-slick canal by a splintery wooden pier.

Midgette drove onto the bridge to Manteo, named for William B. Umstead, who'd been governor in the 1950s as the bridge of more than two miles was built in response to the growing tourist trade, replacing the Croatan Sound ferry that had been the link just a decade before. Cool salt air hit you, and there was shimmering water stretching for miles on either side until it kissed the sky at the horizon. There were seagulls dipping and soaring, cackling over fishermen in boats far below. And then you hit the highest point on the bridge, forty-five feet over the sound. You could see the clouds climbing over wooded shorelines on either side, pocked by docks and sand beaches and, straight down so far below, the water.

Brenda knew about lakes, not sounds. Shotgun Holland had scrimped and saved to get his family a trailer at Lake Glenville, farther up in the mountains from their Canton hometown. But this Croatan Sound was water like Brenda had never seen, wide and free.

They came off the bridge, leaving behind the mainland and old ways, and rode onto the island.

"Seasons of Loss"

Can you picture what will be?
So limitless and free

—*"The End," a song released by The Doors in January 1967*

On a map, Roanoke Island looks like some kind of holy afterthought, a dot cast down between the mainland and the Outer Banks. The island, about ten miles long and three miles wide at its thickest points, is bounded on the west by that Croatan Sound that Brenda crossed, on the east by the Roanoke Sound, on the north by the Albemarle Sound and on the south by the Pamlico Sound. The island floats out there between the sounds of the sea, forever subject to the ocean's moods.

For all the talk about that lost colony, the Algonquian Indians had been on the island first. By the time the English newcomers crashed their party in 1584, the American Indians had been there for generations. Their life was as harsh and hard as it was wild and free, at least for the men. If they had to struggle with disease and early death and swarms of mosquitoes, they also hunted and fished the forests and sounds without answering to despots. They lived in thatch huts and grilled fish over open fires. They wore necklaces made of seashells and danced under the summer moon.

That all began to end in July 1584, when Philip Amadas and Arthur Barlow led an expedition from England that landed on the island. They soon met an Algonquian Indian named Manteo, who was a member of the Croatan tribe. It must have been the ultimate culture clash under a burning summer sun: the barely clad Manteo meeting the heavily clad Englishmen, the Indian trying to figure out the white men as hard as they were trying to figure him out. Manteo—out of curiosity or practicality, or some mix of the two and something else—befriended the Englishmen. "Manteo acted as guide, interpreter and diplomat as the English explored, annotated and interacted with this new world and its people," Angel Ellis Khoury writes in *Manteo: A Roanoke Island Town*. "Not only did he familiarize the English explorers with his world; he traveled across the ocean to learn of theirs. Manteo and another Algonquian, Wanchese, visited England from September 1584 to April 1585, living at least part of the time at the home of Sir Walter Raleigh, and seen at Elizabeth's court 'dressed up in brown taffeta in the English fashion.'" Manteo might have taken note of the thousands packed into London, realizing that there was no end to the waves of white people coming to his shores and beyond.

For his part, Raleigh was constantly calculating—sometimes coolly, sometimes not so much. That writer and man of action was forever fawning to Queen Elizabeth. He explored far and wide and led in establishing the colony on Roanoke Island, but he never set foot in what is now North Carolina, much less on the island. He did, however, orchestrate a 1587 expedition of colonists to the island, following up on two previous, short-lived efforts there. The more than one hundred colonists included John White, the governor of the colony; his daughter Eleanor and her husband, Ananias Dare; and children and other women and men.

The colonists soon began the backbreaking work of setting up the most ambitious English settlement in the New World thus far, one twenty years before the Jamestown, Virginia settlement and thirty years before the Plymouth Rock, Massachusetts one. As the work continued, Manteo was christened, followed eleven days later by the christening of Virginia Dare, the daughter of Ananias and Eleanor.

Manteo might have felt as constrained as John White felt free. White had sketched images of Native Americans like Manteo, scenes of the Indians celebrating the harvest in a circular dance, eating hominy off large round trays and fishing with dipnets and spears from dugout canoes. The pictures are idyllic, oblivious to the hell looming. The Roanoke settlers clashed with Manteo's tribesmen. With supplies running low, White sailed for England to restock. England was warring with Spain. White didn't get back until 1590. His colony had vanished. White and his company had only one big clue to go on: the word *CROATOAN*, carved into a post, and *CRO*, carved into a tree, as most North Carolina schoolchildren, along with many others nationwide, learned. Croatoan, now spelled "Croatan," was the name of Manteo's tribe of the Algonquian. It was also the Indian name of an area of another Outer Banks island, now called Hatteras.

The colonists may well have gone off with Croatan Indians and assimilated into their tribe, but the mystery has never been definitively solved. Maybe Sir Walter Raleigh could have gotten answers. But by then, Raleigh, whom Queen Elizabeth had knighted in 1585, was falling out of favor with the queen for marrying one of her ladies in waiting without her prior approval. After Elizabeth died, in 1603, Raleigh got on the wrong side of King James when his men, searching for El Dorado, the "City of Gold," in South America, warred with Spaniards, violating the treaty with England. King James ordered Raleigh's head sliced off in 1618.

The Lost Colony mystery was the start of "seasons of loss" for the island, as Bland Simpson eloquently put in *The Inner Islands: A Carolinian's Sound Country Chronicle*. The losses included, he wrote, "the Confederates, who nearly three centuries later, encamped on forts on Roanoke, were totally routed by a Federal force that first shelled them from gunboats on Croatan Sound, then stomped through the Roanoke marshes and swamps and came upon them and won for the Union its first major victory in February 1862." Simpson continued with the losses:

> [T]he scores of runaway slaves drawn to the victorious federal force, who made for themselves a freedmen's colony on the island's north end between Weir's and Pork Points, till they were dispossessed of it and lost it two years after the Civil War. If ever there was a place in America that claimed loss as its theme, has long had loss playing its bass line, and has long held fast to loss whether it wanted to or not, Roanoke Island is it. We are haunted forever by all of it, by all these disappearances and undoings, from the distant past and the not-so-far-off as well.

Roanoke had made it through all that, as well as hurricanes, fires, flooding and the Great Depression. It was an isle of survivors. That's the Manteo Brenda entered on that last day of May 1967. As they neared the end of the bridge, Darrell Midgette would have told Brenda that her new worksite was to the left, the soundside theater where *The Lost Colony* had been staged since the Great Depression, when resilient locals had jumpstarted their town, first doing a short film on the lost colony and then enlisting Paul Green to write the play.

Green's play opened in the summer of 1937. In August of that year, President Franklin Roosevelt visited. He was driven down the streets of Manteo, aristocratically tailored and relaxed in the back seat of a luxury convertible with his cigarette holder clenched in his grin, waving to an adoring crowd, his wheelchair discreetly tucked in the car's boot in keeping with the coverup of his polio-induced disability. His Works Progress Administration had helped *The Lost Colony* get started. There was one minor bur: FDR, instead of dining in Manteo, lunched at Nags Head in a big old cedar-shake place by the sea called "the Buchannan Cottage." There was a bit of tension between Manteo, the county seat of the hardworking year-round residents of Dare County, and the landed gentry from the cotton and peanut plantations of northeastern North Carolina who summered in Nags Head cottages called "the Unpainted Aristocracy" for the lack of paint over their cedar-shake siding. The aristocrats lounged on the wraparound porches of those cottages, sipping iced toddies rendered by their Black servants.

As he drove Brenda toward town on U.S. 64, Darrell might have pointed out, to Brenda's left, Mother Vineyard Road, stretching back to the Roanoke Sound, where the well-off folks lived in the shade of live oak trees, dramatically short with widespread branches and deep sand roots. Mother Vineyard Road ended in wondrous views of the Roanoke Sound and, across that sparkling water, over in Nags Head, the yellow sand mountain, Jockey's Ridge, rising more than one hundred feet into the sheltering sky.

Approaching the downtown area, Darrell could have pointed out, to the right, Burnside Road, named after Union general Ambrose Burnside, who led in the capture of the island during the Civil War. The term "sideburns" was said to come from a flip of his name, although his side hair was more like kudzu, starting at his ears and meeting on his chin. Burnside Road was on the border between African Americans and whites in Manteo. The road was part of "Goat Town" and white. Right beside it was "California," one of the two Black areas of Manteo.

Finally, Darrell turned left off U.S. 64 and onto Manteo's short Main Street, which ended at Shallowbag Bay. They passed a few houses before Darrell pulled up in front of a whitewashed frame one where Brenda would rent a room for the summer. It was the home of Dick and Cora Gray Twiford and their children. Dick worked for the state ferry system; was the janitor for his church, Mount Olivet Methodist, for a modest salary; and cut grass as well. Cora ran the house, and she and her two young daughters, Penny and Debbie, played colonists in *The Lost Colony*. Penny was also a flower girl and page for the queen, and her sister was a page as well. Cora Twiford, sweet and mothering, known to cook plates of fried chicken and other food for neighbors sick or otherwise in need, met Brenda and welcomed her.

As Darrell pulled away, Cora Twiford would have showed Brenda around the house, starting with the first floor, the living room up front, the dining room off to the side, the kitchen in the back. Then she would have showed Brenda her efficiency apartment on the second floor. In the front of the apartment were two twin beds, neatly made up—one for her and one for her roommate for the summer, Molly Black, a student from the University of North Carolina–Chapel Hill who would also be working at *The Lost Colony*. In the rear was a small kitchen.

Brenda listened to the Twifords' stories and regaled them with some of her own about growing up in the shade of Holland Mountain with her close-knit clan. When she headed upstairs for bed, she might have written a letter to her parents and maybe read a bit from that novel she had brought from Campbell, *Zorba the Greek*, about an ingénue following an elder into trouble. She could have looked out from her front window onto Main Street, taking in a livelier scene than the one she knew from her college town or her hometown. On the street, members of the *Lost Colony* crew were walking, talking and laughing, high on beer or just life, loving their break from studying and teaching in cloistered college burgs, anticipating making Paul Green's characters all their own and dreaming of making it big from the play, like Andy had. Cars rolled by them, some still with '50s fins and loud tailpipes, headlights breaking the night. Residents of varied ages and races rode around Manteo, guzzling beer late into the night, ranging from bored teenagers just looking for something, anything, to do to a wife fleeing her husband's fists. They'd ride across the bridge to Nags Head, maybe hitting a bar or two, then they'd cruise back to Manteo and ride around some more, anything to put off the end of the night and the start of their workaday world—cleaning fish with dead eyes, typing and manning cash registers, banging endless nails to build cottages for newcomers flush with money they'd never see. Their nights were long and could get mean—the flip side of the peaceful picture the island presented to the outside world.

Lost in Her Colony

They farm, hunt, fish, do Coast Guard work—all sorts of things—and in the summer put on the play and take care of the people who come to see it….I mean a theater in which plays are written, acted, and produced for and by the people.

—*Paul Green, the playwright of* The Lost Colony, *writing in the introduction of his book version of the play published in 1946*

The next afternoon, Brenda caught a ride to her new workplace. In the more than two decades since its playwright had penned those words, the play's working crew had changed. Tourists poured into Manteo and the rest of Dare County for the play, which had for thirty years been ramping up its status as transformative entertainment. It had become a way of life. Many locals were still in it, both in the cast and in support jobs, ranging from adults working the ticket booth to teenagers laboring as ushers. But more and more outsiders were joining the cast for the career connections they could make. The islanders and the outsiders made modest wages. The local businesses reaped the real monetary benefits. The previous season, that of 1966, more than 145,000 people bought tickets for the play, bringing their business to hotels, restaurants and shops.

The Waterside Theater was just a few miles from Brenda's boardinghouse, but it was centuries back in time. The theater was adjacent to Fort Raleigh on National Park Service land, a lush setting that included dense pines and the expansive Elizabethan Gardens with its white and pink begonias sheltered by crepe myrtle trees. There were squat live oak trees more than four hundred years old, their widespread and stone-hard, hurricane-forged branches stretching toward the sound, thick forearms from another time keeping guard even now and carrying stories of old. No one could say for sure exactly where on the island the lost colony had been. But you could stand on the theater grounds and know that colony was still somewhere close.

Brenda checked in at the front desk and was shown backstage. Locals and theater hands from the island and nationwide were trying out dialects and dances, transforming themselves into colonists and Indians. For Brenda, the women playing the American Indians were one thing to watch, but the men, brawny in breechclouts, were something else. This was the big time, a mind-stretching leap from her college plays.

She soon met her new boss, costumer Irene Smart "Renie" Rains. Brenda was a bit in awe. A Wanchese native, Rains had left home and made it big. In the off season, Rains was the costume director of the Carolina Playmakers at the University of North Carolina–Chapel Hill, a post she had held for twenty-five years. Brenda's college drama department was nothing in comparison to the venerable Playmakers, which had nurtured Green, Thomas Wolfe and Andy Griffith.

In 1938, the second season of *The Lost Colony*, Rains came home for the summer and joined the company. She kept coming back. When a fire destroyed the theater, Rains saved nearly all the costumes and had them ready to go by the time the theater was rebuilt. Andy Griffith sometimes stopped by *The Lost Colony* to pay homage to Rains. She was a constant in his life and those of many others. When the spring semester ended in Chapel Hill, Rains moved into her cottage just down the Roanoke Sound beach from the theater.

Rains, often with her hair in a scarf, had kind eyes and a warm smile. She was a perfectionist and the company matriarch. She came down on employees slacking in their jobs or misbehaving away from work. She knew all. She was gentle and compassionate in her execution. She confided to friends that she had "a third eye," an ability to anticipate trouble and try to beat it. She kept contact with her charges years past their time at the colony, advising, cajoling, telling one who got discouraged not to give up on his New York dreams. Rains often gave Brenda rides to and from work. Brenda was soon confiding in her about her differences with her parents. She didn't want to end up like them, fighting and stuck in their hometown.

Brenda got to know other *Lost Colony* members as well. At the top was director and choreographer Joe Layton, towering and handsome with angular features and dark, swept-back hair, given to calling women "dahling" with a borrowed southern accent. At thirty-six, he was well over six feet tall. He was born Joseph Lichtman and grew up in Brooklyn, embracing theater from early on. He worked in choreography and directed musicals in an Army Special Services unit, then made his way on Broadway and in TV, working with Julie Andrews, Carol Channing, Mary Tyler Moore, Carol Burnett and Barbra Streisand and winning Tony and Emmy Awards.

Emma Neal Morrison, the chairwoman of the group that put on *The Lost Colony*, the Roanoke Island Historical Association, had a few years ago recruited Layton to rejuvenate the play. He brought a Broadway shimmer to it. On the cover of the 1967 program, magazine-sized and dwarfing Broadway's *Playbill*, Queen Elizabeth is hip, jewels weaved into her bouffant auburn hair, fan in hand, coolly serene in front of the Waterside Theater and the sound behind it.

Layton was brilliant and charismatic, bringing out the best in his cast, pacing and coaching, occasionally nipping a bit of vodka. He was proud of his exotic and charming actress/wife, Evelyn Russell, and their baby son. He could live and work anywhere in the world he chose, but he loved Manteo and its people. He was as fun-loving as a pirate, meeting his local buddies for breakfast at the Duchess of Dare restaurant, regaling them with ribald stories. He might have talked about his women in New York and Hollywood, but probably not about the men he'd bedded as well. The islanders knew all anyway. They knew that if they were in New York and needed a guide or just help in general, Layton would be there for them.

The locals' acceptance of Layton spoke volumes about their nonjudgmental way of life. The islanders had long accepted that marriage was not necessarily sacred and that there would be gay and bisexual relationships. The *Lost Colony* company, with its free-living members, reinforced that mindset. Gay and bisexual islanders departing for supposedly progressive cities were jarred to find that the rest of the world was not as accepting as their island.

Aycock Brown, the middle-aged news director for the show, was always smiling, constantly taking photos of the cast and ending spurts of conversation with "Don't you see"—not as a question, just as a statement, or at least a brief pause in his word torrent. He was a crane of a man, rail thin and bespectacled with a pencil-thin mustache, often dressed in a Panama hat and a Hawaiian shirt, with two or three big cameras hanging from worn leather straps around his stringy neck and a cigarette dangling from his lips as he cruised Dare County in his big Chevy with the "Aycock" license plate. He was also the county tourism director, pressing buddies nationwide to run

PAUL GREEN'S

The Lost Colony

Concordia: parva crescunt

1967 OFFICIAL SOUVENIR PROGRAM — ONE DOLLAR

The Lost Colony program of 1967. *Author's personal collection.*

his photos of the Outer Banks. He was beloved, known for always helping people whenever he could.

Aycock helped make the play tick. So did another beloved bedrock local, Cora Mae Basnight. She had played the American Indian character Agona for a decade after years of other roles in the play and local venues. As the love-struck Agona, she supplied a popular comic interlude, along with Tommy Hull as the English underdog "Old Tom." Andy Griffith was her trusted friend. Dignitaries, including President Johnson's wife, Lady Bird, sought her out for meet-and-greets backstage. She was happier just showing rank-and-file friends around backstage.

Brenda also got to know the children and teenagers in the company. One of them was David Payne, a thirteen-year-old who sold seat cushions to audience members. He reminded Brenda of her little brother, Charles. A Manteo family had taken David in as a foster child through the county department of social services and then adopted him. He loved the *Colony* crew and was talkative beyond his years, serious and kind, constantly asking his elders questions, finding a sense of belonging with them. He'd had rheumatoid arthritis when he was younger and, consequently, was an islander who couldn't swim. Over at the Nags Head beach, Brenda taught him how. "Hang in there. You'll be all right," she told him as she guided his sea strokes.

Then there were Brenda's contemporaries. There was her roommate, Molly Black, a rich man's daughter who was fun-loving and temperamental. Black was a costume assistant and dancer for the drama.

Brenda's love life soon came to revolve around the show. When she first got to Manteo, she went out a few times with Darrell Midgette, her friend from Campbell who had introduced her to his island hometown. But as June progressed, she dated an actor in the play.

Then she dated Danny Barber, a dark-haired chorus singer. He'd been in the U.S. Army band and was now attending Carolina. In a play built on music, Barber, a tenor in his third season, was a big deal, one of several singers featured in photos in the play program. He was short-haired and earnest in his photo and serious in his singing but fun-loving in all other pursuits, with a flair for casual but stylish clothes, confident in his easy strength, talent and charm. Barber and Brenda rode around in his white Corvair, listening to the car radio and talking.

Both came from families of limited means in small North Carolina towns. They both had big dreams—just like Andy Griffith, who had taught at Barber's high school in Goldsboro, albeit a few decades before Barber attended. Barber and Brenda would have liked Andy's egalitarian view of Manteo and *The Lost Colony*. Years later, he would say, "I struggled all my young life to get out of Mount Airy. When I first came here in '47, I had been 'second class' all my life in Mount Airy, and Chapel Hill was a class-conscious place. I came here [to *The Lost Colony* and Manteo]—all of us lived in this solitary place—and it was classless. All of us who were colonists and singers and all that—it didn't matter where we came from—we were classless. And that was the first thing that attracted me to this place. We all had an equal opportunity; we all started from the same place," Angel Ellis Khoury reports in *Manteo: A Roanoke Island Town.*

Brenda's relationship with Barber was not exclusive. She dated a few other men and told Renie that she believed one of them, Rob Breeze, was trying to take advantage of her. Renie knew of Breeze and advised caution, especially in dates that went past 11:00 p.m. Brenda told her she could handle him.

When not on dates, Brenda and Molly Black hung out, rolling into the Outer Banks night, although Brenda didn't roll as hard as Black. They could ride, as the locals put it, "up the beach," stopping for beers at the Drafty

Brenda (*in left background*) on the Nags Head beach in the summer of 1967. *Courtesy Kim Holland Thorn.*

Tavern, a dive bar on the sound just before the bridge to Nags Head. At the Drafty, commercial fishermen just in from long tours at sea, still in their white rubber boots baptized in fish blood ("Wanchese slippers"), would be blowing wads of greenbacks, their share of the seafood haul, on oceans of beer. Outsiders knew that it was best not to make eye contact with them if they didn't want a fight. There'd be enough fights among the fishermen. The *Colony* crowd and folks of all types from Manteo hung out at the Drafty, talking over cold beer, staring out at the changing moods of the sound, playing tunes on the jukebox and shooting pool under clouds of cigarette smoke. Folks from up the beach, both vacationers and locals, also drank at the Drafty. You could perch on a worn barstool and see both the lights of Manteo and those of the Nags Heads soundside, whiling away the hours, drinking and dreaming.

Driving across the bridge into Nags Head, Brenda and her friends could go to the Casino, a frame building painted white and yellow right across the road from Jockey's Ridge where barefoot dancers—and occasional fights—rocked the second-story dance floor. Ras Westcott of Manteo had bought the place thirty years ago, the year *The Lost Colony* opened, and soon put it on the map by booking bands such as Duke Ellington and Tommy Dorsey. Louis Armstrong played there as well. By Brenda's summer on the Outer Banks, the casino was booking beach music bands such as Bill Deal and the Rhondels and Doug Clark and the Hot Nuts. Their music shook the building and drifted out the open windows, tantalizing young teenagers not old enough to be admitted to the second floor. They'd drift inside to the first floor to bowl and try to use fake IDs to get upstairs.

Up there, crew-cut bouncers with tattooed arms and big bellies bulging out of their T-shirts kept order, tossing long-haired rowdies out. Preppies and locals clashed over girls. Blood sometimes flowed. Men would spit out teeth during fistfights. Fingers—and sometimes ears—would be bitten.

Nags Head police chief Donnie Twyne Sr. (pronounced "Twoine" by the locals), along with Wescott and his bouncers, broke up the fights. They knew what was happening in the big cities, where many in the anti-establishment didn't trust law enforcement. Some of the "long hairs" called lawmen "pigs" and "the fuzz," the latter a slur against their short hair and faces devoid of any hair save, in their eyes, for tiny sprouts.

Just five years before, the Casino had survived the disastrous Ash Wednesday storm, when the ocean and sound had met for miles along the narrow Outer Banks. Wescott would see that it survived this generational storm as well.

On the quieter side, just across the new bypass from the Casino, members of the *Colony* company and their dates climbed Jockey's Ridge barefoot, stared at the moon and sketched dreams in the sand. Later, they headed back to Manteo for parties at spots like the Hill House, where several company members lived, including one Brenda had dated. The Hill House "was a rickety old house high on a dune near the sound just north of Camp Seatone on the North End," as my prologue host would remember years later. "It was far enough away from town that the stodgy old folks could neither see nor hear them. It was the favored place for a late-night party." After long parties, visitors sometimes crashed on worn-out sofas at the cottage.

There were other, more quiet party spots in Manteo. One was the place Danny Barber shared with two other men. It was a two-story wooden house on Burnside Road. Earl Charles Mirus Jr., a Duke University graduate student in forestry, rented the house that season and sublet rooms to Barber and Rodney Perkins Brett, an excitable navy veteran from Virginia's nearby Tidewater region who worked at Nags Head's Carolinian Hotel, a majestic, flat-topped building of stone that shimmered out of the blond dunes like something out of Old Cuba. The folks who ran the oceanfront hotel catered to their fellow aristocracy from northeastern North Carolina, as well as the folks from Manteo and tourists who came to the hotel's Anchor Room to hear music. In those days before liquor by the drink, brown-bagging ruled, with patrons bringing in their favorite booze and paying a set-up fee, a couple of dollars for ice, mixer and glasses. Patrons would spill out of the bar and fall into rattan sofas in the hallways to snuggle. The knotty pine walls of the old hotel held their secrets.

Brett was twenty-eight, older than his two housemates, who were in their mid-twenties. He was fun-loving, tall and thin, with honey-brown hair. He liked interior decorating and was into poems. Women loved him.

Mirus was a cool and wiry man with bright-red hair. He was doing an internship with the West Virginia Pulp and Paper Company (Westvaco) and drove a 1960, candy apple red MG convertible. By day, he ventured out to Westvaco's vast holdings in the woods of mainland Dare County, studying the pine trees and their growth. He was a Catholic boy with a wry sense of humor. He was also a revolver marksman who outshot Manteo police chief C.C. Duvall on an outing with him. On another day, way out there in the swampy woods of the Dare mainland, Mirus pulled his .22-caliber revolver and drew a bead on the neck of a rising rattlesnake, neatly severing its head from its writhing body and later making the snakeskin into a band for a hat.

Brenda *(far right)* with friends in Manteo in the summer of 1967. *Courtesy Kim Holland Thorn.*

By night, Mirus took it easy. He and Brett lived downstairs in the Burnside Road place. Barber lived upstairs. They had small parties. Members of the *Lost Colony* company, locals and seasonal workers would gather in the den with its psychedelic posters on the walls. They'd play music and sing, with Barber often strumming a banjo. They'd pass around jugs of cheap wine and go from folk music to beach music to rock-and-roll, from playing and singing the music themselves to listening to the stereo system. They'd dance. Brett was one of the best dancers, shagging into a sweat with the girls. Brenda had been to those parties.

Early on the Friday night of June 30, at the Twiford house, Brenda prepared for work. She had a date with Barber planned for after the show. A date with Rob Breeze about a week before, their third, had not gone well. Breeze, a former college football player, was in his mid-twenties and divorced. He worked in a beach business his family owned. He was confident with a big smile, a smooth talker with blue eyes and short black hair held in place by Brylcreem, favoring short sleeves that showcased his muscles. He'd taken Brenda to his apartment. What happened there devastated her. Just a few days before, on Wednesday, she'd told Renie Rains, "I'm no good." Rains told her that wasn't true and tried to cheer her up. Brenda said she wasn't going to see Breeze anymore. She told Rains that Breeze continued to pursue her, coming by her boardinghouse once and having his friend Houston Rob Waters try to intercede for him in phone calls to the house. She hadn't gone out one night because she didn't want to run into Breeze. Brenda kept pushing him away.

Brenda in one of her publicity shots for *The Lost Colony*. *Courtesy Kim Holland Thorn.*

By Friday night, she was rebounding. The opening week of the play had gone well. She had kept up with the pace and pressure of the shows. She was becoming enamored of island life, including the easy and familiar respect the locals held for one another, with the young adults calling their elders by their first names, but always with a respectful "Mr." or "Miss" tacked on up front, as in "Mr. John" or "Miss Jane." The islanders were beginning to trust her, telling her their stories in their alluring brogue. They took note of all things, and they saw how she had taken in the boy David Payne, the young *Colony* worker, and taught him to swim. The locals were granting her entrance into a world into which they allowed few outsiders. Brenda was beginning to see that almost everyone on that spot of sand was, at least, a distant cousin. Some islanders laughingly said that was because, until the last several years, there had been no ferries. They joked that they welcomed the *Colony* outsiders whom they accepted, occasionally marrying into their clans, because it kept them from bearing children with six toes on a single bare foot.

Brenda loved the changing moods of the sea and sounds and the way the islanders could sense storms moving in long before the sketchy weather reports on the radio or TV. She also liked the stories from the "wash-ins," like her, the way they were casting aside their old lives and crafting new ones in a place where they could be themselves.

The *Colony* company, she knew, was its own subculture on the island, an enclave whose members stood up for one another, just as the lost colonists had done all those centuries before. Renie Rains had taken her in and made her feel better about herself, accepted in her new world.

The next weekend, Brenda would celebrate her twentieth birthday. She had just written her parents a letter saying how much she loved her work and Manteo, teasing that they needed to come down and "see how real people live."

She dressed for work. She put on a teddy with a leopard-skin pattern, a nod to the artsy world in which she was feeling more and more comfortable. She pulled over it a maroon skirt and zipped it up. Then she donned a multicolored blouse. She selected her favorite piece of jewelry, the silver necklace she'd won back home the previous summer for being named Miss Congeniality in the local beauty pageant. She slipped on her brown sandals, size 7, gave her newly blond hair a quick look and grabbed her big blue-and-white canvas handbag with its braided rope handle. Tucked in it were her cosmetics and *Zorba the Greek*.

She glided down the steps and out the front door, ready for work.

"An Ungodly Scream"

Alas I'm not a tiny sparrow;
I have not wings nor can I fly
And on this earth in grief and sorrow
I am bound until I die.

—Brenda Holland's handwritten transcription of a lyric from "Tiny Sparrow,"
a 1963 song performed by the folk trio Peter, Paul and Mary

On Saturday, July 1, *The Lost Colony* was kicking off with its opening lines, a prayer:

…We ask the witness of Thy grace
Upon this sacred spot,
This bit of humble earth
Which we have come to dedicate.
For here once walked the men of dreams,
The sons of hope and pain and wonder,
Upon their foreheads truth's bright diadem,
The light of the sun their countenance,
And their lips singing a new song—
A song for ages yet unborn,
For us the children that came after them…

In the audience, as moonbeams danced across the backdrop of the Roanoke Sound, some children would soon be fascinated, and others terrified, by the American Indians on stage. Many of their parents would enjoy the play. Some of the adults would keep checking their wristwatches, yawning and yearning for the favor of the performance's end in a few hours, dreaming of nightcaps and bed. Everybody would be swatting at mosquitoes and sweating, using their magazine-sized playbills to fan their faces.

Backstage, the *Colony* crew had a real worry: Brenda was missing. Actors and actresses dressed as Indians and colonists drank Coca-Colas from pony bottles, smoked cigarettes and talked, corralling one another into corners and whispering. If this were another girl, they might not be so concerned. But Brenda was not wild. She had never missed a day of work at the pageant. Cora Twiford, her landlady who played a colonist in the show, had noted that she hadn't come in the night before. Brenda's roommate, Molly Black, had returned about 7:00 a.m. that morning after being out all night, and Twiford had overheard Black on the hallway phone telling a friend that Brenda had not come home. It wasn't unusual for some boarders to stay out all night, Twiford knew, but it was unusual for Brenda. Most of her possessions were still in her room.

Twiford voiced her concerns to Renie Rains, who in turn told John Fox, the general manager of the play. By midway through the show, Fox, a middle-aged transplant from the state capital of Raleigh who'd served in the navy during World War II, was pacing backstage. An intense man with glasses and a receding hairline, he was chain-smoking. There might have been no secrets in Manteo, but there surely were none among the *Colony* crew. The night before, after the Friday show, Renie Rains and others had taken note of Danny Barber and Brenda leaving the theater parking lot for a date, pulling away in Barber's Corvair. Fox mulled that over as the first act of the two-act play ended with the English colonists walking to the ship that would bring them to Roanoke Island.

As intermission began, Fox pulled Barber aside and pressed him on the matter backstage. He leaned in close, his cigarette smoke streaming in Barber's face, and asked a question: When was the last time you saw Brenda?

"About 2:00 a.m. this morning," Barber replied. "I let her out in front of her house."

Cora Twiford, always good and honest, looking even more forthright in her colonist dress that flowed to the floor, was standing nearby. She spoke right up. "That's not true, Danny," she told him. "Brenda didn't come home last night."

"Well, Mr. Fox," Barber said, "Mrs. Twiford is right. Brenda and I went back to my house after a night out at Nags Head. We went up to my room and we talked while lying on my bed. I fell asleep, and when I woke up about dawn today, Brenda was gone. I just figured she walked home."

The second act was starting. The chat ended.

Rains told Fox to call Rob Breeze at his business. Breeze, sounding alarmed, said he hadn't seen Brenda in a week or more.

At 9:20 p.m., Fox called the sheriff's office to report Brenda missing. He hung out backstage for the rest of the play, listening closely to the worried chats among Brenda's co-workers. The play ended, as always, with the colonists vanishing into the island darkness. Fox hurried to his car and drove to the sheriff's office to drop off programs that included Brenda's photo. The office was in the Dare County Courthouse, a 1904 brick building with white columns in the center of downtown Manteo, right across from Shallowbag Bay. *Lost Colony* playwright Paul Green, islanders and congressmen had met in that courthouse as they sketched out plans for their play in advance of the 1937 premiere.

Thirty years later, Deputy Will Daniels, manning the desk, was busy with calls reporting fights and scrambling through the headache of paperwork for deputies checking drunks into the adjacent jail. But he caught the importance of Fox's mission and found time to hand the programs out to his fellow officers so they could be on the lookout for Brenda. Fox went home but couldn't sleep. At 6:00 a.m. Sunday morning, he called the sheriff's office. "I'm worried about this girl," he told the dispatcher.

The dispatcher was used to similar concerns from ordinary citizens. She knew not to bother her boss on Sunday mornings, when Cahoon liked to be in his regular seat at Manteo Baptist Church. But the dispatcher knew that Fox was no ordinary citizen. He was the head of *The Lost Colony*, the town's money stream. The dispatcher picked up her phone and called Cahoon. The sheriff skipped church that Sunday.

FRANK CAHOON WAS A taut man of sixty years. He was one of several children of a farmer from mainland Dare County. After high school, he worked at a shipyard in Norfolk, Virginia, and a dairy on Roanoke Island. He once said that he knew nothing about law enforcement when he won election in 1946 but was determined to learn all he could. For two weeks every January for more than fifteen years, he attended law enforcement seminars at the Institute of Government at the University of North Carolina–Chapel Hill. He was moderately progressive, having kept on his staff a female deputy—the county's first—whom he'd inherited from his predecessor.

He spoke the Outer Banks brogue in a soft but assured voice. He had a long nose, crow's feet around his intense dark eyes and gray hair combed back and parted near the middle. After the dispatcher called him Sunday morning, he pulled out of his driveway in his red-and-white Ford cruiser. The car was as low-key as its driver. It didn't proclaim "Dare County High Sheriff" on its side. It did have a whip antenna on the rear bumper, the permanent government license plate in back and a small black-and-white tag up front that said "SHERIFF."

Cahoon lived on U.S. 64, the main road running through Manteo, within a few miles of the *Colony* theater and his office. On the other side of the main drag was the entrance to the soundside home of Andy Griffith. Cahoon was accustomed to reality colliding with myth. He and Griffith were friends. Like the TV sheriff, Cahoon rarely carried a gun on himself, although he did carry one in his patrol car. Sheriff Taylor wore a khaki uniform and a badge. Sheriff Cahoon usually dressed in street clothes without his badge in plain sight. He was a bit tougher than Sheriff Taylor—Cahoon once said that, in his early days on the job, he didn't need a gun because he could out-wrestle most of the men he had to arrest, the moonshiners and drunks the rural sheriffs of the time had to conquer to stay elected.

On an island anchored on a play with a TV star from that play in residence, Cahoon, if only subconsciously, pushed for his own starring role. Aycock Brown made sure of it. His published photos never caught the sheriff looking vulnerable, but always vigilant, often with his civilian fedora tipped, his dark eyes fierce. Cahoon was rugged, but critics said he was more of a politician than an investigator.

That Sunday morning at 7:30 a.m., the sheriff met John Fox. They sat across from each other in Cahoon's tidy office in the courthouse. The sheriff took an electric coffee pot from his windowsill and poured coffee into Styrofoam cups. Fox, chain-smoking, was about to jump out of his skin over the disappearance of this girl. The sheriff had not met Brenda. But the more Cahoon listened to his friend, the more he realized there was indeed cause for concern about Brenda's failure to show for work and Barber saying he had taken her home and then admitting he had not. Cahoon took a pad and pen from his shirt pocket and took notes. Fox gave Cahoon Barber's address.

"I'll go pick up Danny," Cahoon told Fox. "I'll bring him back to your office in a bit."

The sheriff walked outside and climbed into his cruiser. He had four full-time deputies to patrol a county of more than 1,500 square miles, from the Alligator River bridge leading into mainland Dare to Hatteras Island to the Currituck County line north of the miniscule town of Duck. Every year, the Dare County population swelled like a Saturday-night black eye, from 7,500 in the winter to 50,000 in the summer. Cahoon must have known somewhere down deep that the whole state and beyond would be watching this case, putting his carefully crafted career on the line.

The sheriff drove through town, waving and nodding at some of his constituents, dressed up and walking their children and grandchildren to church on the Sunday sidewalks, women worried about the heat wilting their sprayed hair and makeup and men tugging at their tight neckties. Cahoon knew most of these people, ranging from commercial fishermen to store clerks, by name, and he knew their secrets—who drank too much and who was screwing whose wife or husband. This was his town, his county. He knew every street in Manteo as well as he knew every beat-down fishing camp and yellow-dirt, deer-tracked logging road in the mainland part of the county from which he sprang—the places where, when hunting moonshine stills, he pulled on thick leather boots when walking in the brush among water moccasins. He knew the beach as well, ranging from wild Hatteras Island to Coquina Beach, where the ribs of a shipwreck stood out in the sand.

Many a day, he would ride north, through Whalebone Junction in Nags Head, past the building where Andy Griffith had done his comedy routines late weekend nights after he finished at *The Lost Colony*. Cahoon would roll onto the two-lane asphalt of the Beach Road, passing Sam & Omie's restaurant, started in 1937, the same year *The Lost Colony* began, and Owens' Restaurant, started soon after World War II by friends of his from Manteo.

The sheriff would ride through the desolate Epstein tract, undeveloped sand owned by out-of-towners. Leaving that tract behind, he would ride by the aristocratic Arlington Hotel on the oceanfront and, just across from it on the Beach Road, the Seafare restaurant with which the son of the Arlington owners, "Cap'n" Mike Hayman, was making his own name. The Seafare was an exotic vision, a one-story oasis of pink stucco on blond sand.

Cahoon would drive past the "the Unpainted Aristocracy," old cottages with cedar-shake siding, and the church of their owners, St. Andrew's By the Sea, with the same design. Legend held that, in the early 1900s, when the church needed a door and was short on money, one that perfectly fit the building's dimensions washed up on the nearby beach.

Cahoon would take in the old cottages and the fresh ones that had come in, making the mix eclectic. At Mile Post 10, there was a totally new style of cottage, an A-frame with a stained-glass window on the side like something out of a church. Right beside it was a stucco, flat-roofed cottage painted turquoise, the color of a Bahamian bay, with driftwood guarding it like sea beasts.

The sheriff knew the spots to stop and chat with locals, like the grocery store in Nags Head owned and operated by Carl and Sally Nunemaker. A quarter mile north of that store, just across the Nags Head border in Kill Devil Hills, was the Ocean House motel, a seafront spot of brick and wood with a parking lot circling a pool where families played. Cahoon and fellow Manteo resident Billy Tarkington owned the motel with partners. Tarkington, kin to Cahoon through marriage, was the son of a Manteo store

The author's "Uncle Billy" Tarkington of Manteo (*third from left in this photo*) during his World War II service on board a ship in the South Pacific. After the war, Tarkington, Dare County sheriff Frank Cahoon and partners opened a motel in Kill Devil Hills, the Ocean House, that became the headquarters of the State Bureau of Investigation agents on Brenda's case. The author's father is seated on Tarkington's immediate right. *Author's personal collection.*

owner. Tarkington, balding and erudite, was a World War II navy veteran of the South Pacific who'd been beloved as a teacher at Manteo High School.

Cahoon knew his county's old-line communities as well. He knew the drunks and the straight folks and all in between, the "colored folks" and the racists and the liberals.

He knew the Nags Head Woods, near Jockey's Ridge, that hugged the Roanoke Sound—those woods where locals said a witch surrounded by black cats had held court in the early 1900s, casting a spell of inclement weather on fishermen who did not share with her their harvest. Cahoon knew Kitty Hawk village and the island of the great fishing and battling folk of Colington, just west off Kill Devil Hills, in the shadow of the tall stone memorial to the Wrights, those brothers from Ohio who glided off a tall dune into history with that first flight on a December day in 1903.

Sheriff Cahoon was not an especially introspective sort, but he did know that his county was rapidly changing. In the beach towns, it was all the tourists coming in, more every year. Locals' ancestors, some of whom were shipwreck survivors, had made a sustenance living off fishing, then had jobs with the U.S. Life-Saving Service, the precursor of the Coast Guard. Now they were reaping dollars from the tourist industry, opening restaurants, hotels and charter-fishing businesses. Souvenir shops reaped money for all sorts of things, even driftwood. Some locals were selling sand passed down through their families for generations, lots that not too long ago had been deemed virtually worthless. In the late 1930s, at Milepost 10 in Nags Head, lots just west of the Beach Road could be purchased for $5 each. Two Elizabeth City brothers bought several up until their parents told them they were spending too much money. In the early 1960s, oceanfront cottages in Nags Head could be purchased for less than $20,000. Now the prices were rising. And with all the newcomers and demand for land, the culture was changing.

In Cahoon's Manteo, *The Lost Colony* was the major catalyst. While many residents and families still worked in the show, it was bringing in more and more artsy types from around the country—too many for Cahoon's tastes. He could not get his mind around all the *Colony* folk coming in, as well as other newcomers in general, some of whom became permanent residents. These "wash-ins" were good for business, but they also increased the already heavy workload on his lean department.

THAT SUNDAY, CAHOON DROVE toward Danny Barber's house, turning off U.S. 64 onto Burnside, a road of midsize houses divided by spots of dense woods. The sheriff parked his cruiser in front of Barber's address at about 8:30 a.m. that Sunday morning and got out. Squirrels barked from branches overhead. Cahoon noted two cars parked in the driveway: a 1963 Chevy Corvair, four-door, white in color, and a 1960 Ford Falcon, black in color. He might have touched the hoods of the cars to gauge how recently they had run by their warmth. Cahoon walked up to the front door and gave it a knock.

A lean man in his late twenties answered, opening the door to the man he instantly recognized as the sheriff. Cahoon's stern mug was constantly in photos in the *Coastland Times*, Dare County's only local newspaper, based in Manteo and long run by the Meekins family. The man swallowed hard. Cahoon smiled.

"Hello, son. I'm Sheriff Cahoon. I'm looking for Danny Barber."

"Yes sir, he's not up just yet but I'll wake him. Come on in, Sheriff. What's going on?"

"Just a little somethin'. You just go ahead and wake Danny. Oh, let me ask, what's your name?"

"Rodney Brett. I work at the Carolinian and was just leaving for there."

"That's fine. But do let me get your work number. Y'all don't have a phone here in the house, do you?"

"No sir."

The sheriff pulled a small pad from his left shirt pocket and wrote down Brett's work number. Brett then hustled upstairs to wake Barber. A few minutes later, Brett was out the door, headed for work, and Barber was groggily walking down the stairs, still in his boxer shorts and shirtless. He and Cahoon warily eyed each other. Barber, shorter than the sheriff and more muscular, spoke first.

"Hello, Sheriff. What's the problem?"

"Good morning, Danny. Brenda Holland hasn't been seen since late Friday night. And near as I can tell, you had a date with her that night and were the last person seen with her."

Cahoon stared Barber down, watching him turn pale. Barber ran his hand through his hair and scratched his neatly trimmed beard.

"That's right, Sheriff. We came back here, up to my room. I fell asleep. When I woke up around dawn yesterday morning, she was gone. I figured she must have walked back to the Twifords'. Then I found out last night she didn't get there. I've been worried sick about her."

Danny Barber in the 1967 *Lost Colony* program. *Author's personal collection.*

Barber stared at the sheriff, waiting for him to say something. Cahoon surfed the silence for a moment or two. Finally, he said, "Who else lives here with y'all?"

"Earl Mirus, works for Westvaco. He's gone to see his girlfriend up in New Jersey this weekend."

"All right then. Danny, ride downtown with me if you would and answer a few questions. Go ahead and get dressed, son."

Cahoon drove Barber to Fox's office, in downtown Manteo near the courthouse. They sat down with Fox.

"Any chance Brenda could have gone up north with Mirus, that housemate of yours?" Cahoon asked Barber.

"No sir, Sheriff. They didn't even know each other that well."

Cahoon subtly pressed him for several minutes but couldn't get any more out of Barber. Finally, Barber asked if he was free to go.

"Sure," the sheriff told him.

Barber left. The man's shifts in his story, first saying at *The Lost Colony* that he had driven Brenda home and then admitting he had not, was troubling. Fox said that Barber told him he was scared of Renie Rains. Renie was not slow to let her "boys and girls" know when she disapproved of their behavior.

All the sheriff had was a missing person case. But given Brenda's character, the case was giving both the sheriff and Fox a bad feeling. They made plans. They decided to alert Brenda's parents. The sheriff would organize a search along what would have been Brenda's walk toward home from Barber's house. He and Fox would let reporters know that Brenda was missing in the hope publicity would bring out tips about where she was. And the sheriff would follow up on with Barber's housemates, Earl Mirus and Rodney Brett.

The sheriff was friends with Mirus's boss, Quentin Bell. The sheriff called Bell and told him to let him know when Mirus returned to the island.

That night, Cahoon went by the Carolinian, the Nags Head hotel where Brett worked. Cahoon arranged with Brett's boss to interview Brett in a small office in the hotel. Cahoon led Brett in and had him take a seat. Brett was nervous.

"Tell me about what you saw and heard at your house late Friday night and early Saturday," Cahoon told Brett. Brett gave this statement:

I worked until about 11:30 p.m. As soon as I got off work, I went to the Tap Room [the bar in the oceanfront Nags Header Hotel, on the Beach Road in Nags Head near the Carolinian] *and had three or four beers, as I usually did. Then I came straight home. I went to bed about 1. I had only been in bed a very short time when Danny came in. Danny stopped in the living room only a very short time, then he went upstairs. At first, I thought Danny was alone. There was very little noise and no music, records or radio playing.*

After Danny went upstairs, I heard a woman's voice up in his room. There's a grill vent in the ceiling above my room that goes into the floor of Danny's room. I heard very plainly the voices of Danny and a girl, and heard the bed springs making a lot of noise. I assumed they had sex, or at least assumed that was what was going on because of the noise. I dropped off to sleep and was awakened by what I thought was a cat scratching on the front door screen, but I was sure I heard the front door open and close. But I didn't hear any car start up. I went back to sleep. When I woke up about 7:45 or 8 a.m., I got up and left the house. I was sure that Danny's and Earl's cars were both parked in the yard at about their usual places.

Late Saturday night at our house, Danny and I were talking about Brenda's disappearance. He said, "You do not know it, but I had Brenda here at the house and in my room last night."

I told him, "Yes I did know that you had Brenda in your room last night because I heard both of you upstairs."

Brett ended on this note: "I'm nervous and don't want to stay at that house any longer and have already talked to my boss about it." His statement was problematic. Why was Brett in such a hurry to move out of the house? Was he scared of Barber? Or was he involved in Brenda's disappearance?

CAHOON HAD TROUBLE THAT Sunday reaching Brenda's parents. John Fox had given him a home phone number for them, but no one was answering. By late Sunday afternoon, TV and radio stations, alerted by the sheriff, were broadcasting reports that Brenda was missing and asking for the public's help in finding her. The sheriff gave the media Brenda's photo from *The Lost Colony* program and her general description: five feet, seven inches tall, 120 pounds, short blond hair. He had gathered from Brenda's roommate a description of the clothes she was last seen wearing. But he withheld it, knowing that inside information might help in ferreting out suspects.

Sunday night up in Canton, Brenda's big sister, Ann Holland Earley, heard one of those reports on her AM car radio while she and her husband were driving home from church. Ann was shaken, scared for Brenda, whom she knew to be trusting, maybe too trusting. Her husband, Vernon Earley, drove to the Canton Police Department. The Earleys knew the officer working the front desk. They asked him about what they just heard on the radio. "Oh my gosh," the officer said, "I didn't realize that was your sister. The sheriff down there has been trying to reach your parents. Where are they?"

"They're at their trailer up at Lake Glenville," Ann told the officer. "Somebody's got to let them know. They don't have a phone up there."

"We'll take care of it, Ann," the officer told her. "I'll call the sheriff's office."

A Haywood County deputy was soon on the way up to Lake Glenville, about an hour's drive west of Canton, The trailer on what Brenda's little sister Kim called a "hairpin, kiss-your-tail" road was the family's happy place, where Kim and her brother, Little Charles, played in the woods while their father, "Shotgun," fished in his small boat. The family matriarch, Gerri, afraid of water and wanting no part of getting in a boat, did housework and looked after her flowers.

The family usually stayed up late there, watching the 11:00 p.m. local news on their black-and-white TV with its rabbit ear antennae. But that night, the parents and their youngest children, wiped out from the day's activities, had gone to bed early. They'd had a good day. Gerri had been singing "It's Such a Pretty World Today," a song that Wynn Stewart had taken to top of the country charts that spring. But one part of the day was unusual: the dog Brenda had left behind when she went off to school, a collie/German shepherd mix named Prince, had done nothing all day but pace up and down the long steep driveway leading up the trailer. That calm dog never acted like that. The Hollands couldn't figure out what had gotten into him.

Late that night, someone knocked on the trailer door. Shotgun Holland rolled out of bed wide awake, a habit he had picked up during the war. He knew this could not be good. Visitors were unusual at his remote trailer, especially late at night. He thought about where his .22-caliber revolver was, but then he peeked out a window and saw the Haywood County deputy.

Shotgun wondered what the hell was going on as he cut on a light and made his way to the door. Then he realized that something had happened to his Brenda. Good old reliable Ann was surely safe and sound in Canton with her husband and children. Gerri and his youngest children were in the trailer. But Brenda was down at that god-forsaken Manteo.

Shotgun stepped outside to talk to the deputy. Brenda had been missing for two days and hadn't shown up at work, which was not like her, the deputy said, relaying the news from Dare County. Shotgun pressed the deputy: "Well, what happened to her? What do they think?"

"They just don't know," the deputy said. "They're starting a big search for her."

"All right," Shotgun said. He went back into the trailer. He told Gerri what was going on, that the two of them would go to Manteo, leaving their youngest children with Ann. Little Charles and Kim were up by then. "Kids, you all pack up and do it fast," Shotgun told them. Kim soon climbed in the car with the deputy. He'd lead the way back to Canton. Shotgun, a Kool cigarette hanging from his lips, got into his 1961 Ford Sunliner convertible with his wife and Little Charles. He revved up the white car's big V-8 for the ride down the mountain. The black rag top was up. This was no pleasure cruise.

EARLY THE NEXT MORNING, Monday, as the news that Brenda was missing kept crackling across radio waves and flashing across fuzzy TV screens in Manteo, a team of about seventy-five searchers started their work, moving through the thick woods between the houses on Burnside Road. They were Brenda's fellow members of the *Lost Colony* company, joined by a couple of Cahoon's deputies. The sweating volunteers, some hungover, swatted at mosquitoes and pushed through the briars that tore their skin. Many company members had family and friends coming for the holiday week. Some had already arrived. That didn't matter. This was for Brenda. Snakes slithered off as they worked through the brush. The irony was sadly overpowering; people from a play about a colony that vanished in the late 1500s searching for a vanished comrade in the late 1960s. They were hunting something they didn't want to find: Brenda's body.

Island time seems to move slower than mainland time, but not that day. Expectations were fading with the passing of each hot minute. Robert Midgett, who lived about a quarter mile up Burnside Road from Barber's house, told Cahoon Monday morning that before dawn Saturday morning, he heard strange sounds on the road near his frame house. In his official statement, he said that the morning was very hot, so he had his window up:

> *I heard a car come by the house that sounded like it was about to cut off, and, as it passed by my house, it moved slowly a short distance, approximately 120 yards from my house and stopped. After the car had been stopped for approximately three minutes, I heard my neighbor's dog run out to the corner of the yard and growl. I got up out of bed and looked out the window, but the car was too far down the road to see. But I heard a man's voice saying "That dog is a big dog" but I did not hear any answer and the dog did not bark anymore. I looked at my clock and it was 3 a.m. and shortly after that I heard a sound like tools clanging on the road, then everything was silent. There was no sound of any kind for 20 to 30 minutes. Later, I heard a scream like a woman screaming loudly as if she were trying to make an "oh" sound and then silence after that for about twenty to thirty minutes. The next thing I heard was a scraping sound on the hard surface that sounded like a hoe scraping the road, and then everything was silent and a few minutes later, I heard the car start and at this time it was about daylight. It was around 5.*

Midgett was the supervisor of Dare County liquor stores, based in Manteo. He figured again in the case Monday afternoon when George Washington King, described at the time as an illiterate "local Negro," walked into the Manteo store. King, a stocky man of sixty-one, wore a ball cap, an untucked plaid shirt and khakis tucked into his work boots. Midgett overheard King talking to his sales manager as King bought a pint of whiskey. King said he'd found a wallet while driving his lawn-cutting tractor on Scarborough Town Road in Manteo. The sales manager looked at the wallet, saw Brenda's identification in it and told him to take it to the sheriff's office because it belonged to the missing girl. After King left, Midgett hurried out front and consulted with the sales manager. Midgett waited a short while and called the sheriff's office, asking if King had come by and given them the billfold. "We haven't seen him," the dispatcher said.

Midgett told the dispatcher about the sales manager's talk with King. Deputies soon picked up King. He had the small brown wallet, with a small amount of cash still in it. Cahoon sat down in his office with him.

This was a powerful white sheriff in the South of the 1960s confronting a powerless Black man trapped in a precarious situation: having the wallet of a missing white woman and not being in a hurry to turn it in. In many southern counties back then, King would have been done. Cahoon might have initially had some hard words for him. But King held to his story about finding the wallet on Scarborough Town Road. The spot King described was about two miles from Barber's house. Cahoon knew King. King was a binge drinker, but he was harmless, not that much over five feet tall. He had not learned to read before dropping out of school in the fourth grade. He couldn't have known the wallet was Brenda's. Maybe King was protecting somebody, but Cahoon didn't sense that. Instead, the sheriff deduced that King, shaken by what he learned in the liquor store, had chugged much of the pint he purchased and then delayed coming to the sheriff's office, not wanting to get busted for public drunkenness. Instead of going for King, Cahoon just concentrated on extracting from him the exact location where he'd made his find.

"Take a ride with me, George, and show me where you found that wallet."

"Yes sir, Sheriff. Be glad to."

As they walked out of his office, Cahoon told the dispatcher to have a couple of deputies join him at the site to help search it. Once there, King pointed to where he'd found the billfold. On the opposite side of the road, about one hundred feet away from where the billfold was found, deputies collected a blue-and-white canvas shoulder bag with thin rope straps, as well as an eyebrow pencil and comb. Before they could check the area for footprints, the sky fell out in a torrent, ending that possibility.

At the Twiford house, deputies showed the handbag and other items to Brenda's roommate, who identified them as Brenda's. The spot where the items was found was near an asphalt plant and its burrow pond. Cahoon had divers search the pond on the chance that Brenda's body might have been thrown in there. As a crowd gathered and watched, the divers searched in vain for hours.

Cahoon questioned George Washington King no more. The edition of the *Coastland Times* the following Friday all but made King out to be a hero. In a sepia photo, King "points to the spot on the road where he found the purse." The photo taken by Aycock Brown carries a headline of "He Brought Break in Holland Mystery," and the caption reads, "George Washington King, who lives in the California section of Roanoke Island, gave the first clue of possible foul play in the case of missing Brenda Joyce Holland when he reported on Monday that he found a purse with Miss Holland's identification cards."

Soon, Robert Midgett told reporters that the scream he'd heard was an "ungodly" one. Midgett's statement, and his elaborations on it, would become a bedrock of the case but a controversial one. There the strong implication that the woman he heard scream was Brenda and that the scream may have marked the "point of impact" with her killer. The Midgett or Midgette surname, whether with an *e* on the end or without, is a name deeply rooted on the Outer Banks. Their ancestors include heroes of lifesaving teams that went out in all manner of hellish seas, risking their lives to save the crews of some of the hundreds of ships that crashed on the shoals of the "Graveyard of the Atlantic" off the Outer Banks. Robert Midgett cared deeply about *The Lost Colony* and its company, having played a soldier several years before. Renie Rains was among those who liked Midgett. He was a barrel-chested man who loved opera and was always singing, to the point he was known as "Singin' Bob" by some to distinguish him from other Robert Midgetts. Such nicknames were common on the island where several people shared names. Friends found "Singin' Bob" to be excitable, dramatic and maybe even a bit unsteady. His wife, sleeping in another room, said she didn't hear the scream, but she may have been deep asleep. Another neighbor, using racist language common for the times, told investigators she heard screams around that time, but said, "I didn't pay too much attention to them because I often hear screams from the road in front of my house which is traveled considerably by colored people. I've heard screams from the colored section on numerous occasions and pay no attention to those screams."

A Fourth of July filled with contradictions dawned the next day, Tuesday. Up the beach in Nags Head, revelers were preparing for the night. The traffic was already getting heavy, with the mom and pop motels proclaiming "No vacancy" in neon as families frolicked in pools and on the beaches, building sandcastles, bodysurfing and chasing sand fiddlers. The old-line families of the Unpainted Aristocracy, the one-mile strand of cedar-shake cottages, were posting American flags on their wraparound porches. In the last century, these families from northeastern North Carolina had moved from the Roanoke Sound side to the oceanfront. African American servants they brought along were shucking corn and snapping beans, bought from mainland vendors in straw hats who made deliveries in pickup trucks with numerous dents ("love bumps"). Jap Richardson, the head of the lifeguard beach service, was keeping a wary eye on the sea. The Friday before, an eighteen-year-old West Virginia man had drowned in Kitty Hawk, breaking a record—for more than five years, there had not been a water fatality on the Dare beaches.

Manteo was doing business as well. A full-page ad that week in the *Coastland Times* proclaimed:

Manteo Business Firms
Cordially invite you to see
The Lost Colony
And Visit Other Attractions of Interest
On Roanoke Island

Make your headquarters with us, where comfortable accommodations will be found; well-stocked stores can serve your every need; and services are available to make your stay most pleasant.

An investigative team was falling into place. Sheriff Cahoon would soon be joined by five veteran State Bureau of Investigation agents. The SBI often assists local law enforcement agencies with major investigations. The most active of the agents would be Orville Lenwood "Lenny" Wise Sr., who lived in nearby Elizabeth City. Cahoon and Wise, thirty-nine, were old friends and colleagues. Cahoon was more than twenty years older, but they both came from mainland Dare County. Wise, the son of a commercial fisherman, had attended East Carolina Teacher's College and served in the Highway Patrol before coming to the SBI. He was tall and lanky and kept his brown hair short. He had a deep voice and liked to talk, but not too much. Lenny Wise took care of business and was generally unflappable. He drank after work with some members of Manteo's old-line families. Wise, just as Cahoon, spoke in the Outer Banks brogue.

The other members of the team would be SBI agents Dan Gilbert, Jack Thomas and Charlie Ray and Supervisor Clyde Fentress. The agents would set up residence and headquarters at the Ocean House. They would not fit in like Wise. Their four-door sedans were unmarked but easy to spot with their government license plates. The agents stuck out with their clipped cuts, leather briefcases and ties, their suit jackets covering their holstered pistols.

The SBI had been established in 1925. The five agents who would work the case represented about a seventh of the agency's total force. This case would be watched at the highest levels. The agents would soon be copying Myron McBryde, the agency head, on their reports. The *Lost Colony*/Outer Banks connection was already making the case the target of nationwide publicity, but not the kind that beach tourism, a burgeoning bedrock of the state economy, needed. The governor, Democrat Dan K. Moore, was from Brenda's hometown and knew her parents. Moore was a World War II vet who was legal counsel for the mill where Brenda's father worked, the Champion paper company in Canton, until he left to run for governor in 1964. At his inauguration just a few years before, Brenda, playing flute, had marched in Raleigh with her Canton High School band. In an official portrait, Governor Moore, in a dark suit and casually holding in his right hand a cigarette that's almost burned down to his fingers, stares with burning blue eyes. The man did not mess around.

Neither did Brenda's father. By that Tuesday, he was in Manteo, having raced down with his wife and two in-laws the day before in his Ford Sunliner, a model that was a cousin to the Thunderbird. Shotgun Holland was coiled and ready to strike. He came in packing a revolver and a knife, chain-smoking Kool cigarettes and drinking a bit to calm his nerves, out to find his second-oldest daughter or die trying. The Hollands were staying with Renie Rains at her soundfront home near the *Lost Colony* theater but were often at the home of Brenda's landlords, the Twifords, in downtown Manteo. They talked to reporters there Tuesday. Shotgun Holland noted that his daughter had been named "Miss Congeniality" in the local beauty contest the previous year and appeared to be happy with her job in Manteo. Gerri Holland, shorter than her daughter but with her same striking looks, told reporters that Brenda "is the most wonderful girl. A good, Christian girl."

The Hollands were taken aback by Brenda's photo in the *Lost Colony* program. They had no idea she'd dyed her hair blond and cut it short. But her wide-open eyes and big smile, right down to the slight gap between her front teeth, were still very much the Brenda they loved. They could hear her voice and her laughter. And it was killing them.

Shotgun Holland sensed soon after arriving in town that Manteo was as insular as the mountain hollow in which he was raised. He knew the islanders had secrets they were loath to share. But he was damned sure that he would pry out of them anything they knew about his sweet daughter's whereabouts. He walked the streets and popped into restaurants and stores, asking for any word on Brenda's whereabouts.

The searches continued Wednesday as more items, soon identified as Brenda's by her roommate, were found. Lipstick and mascara were discovered along the road leading to the *Lost Colony*'s Waterside Theater, as was Brenda's copy of *Zorba the Greek*, which had tucked into it a prescription for Brenda and a valentine card to Shotgun Holland from a niece of Brenda's. Her sandals were found along U.S. 64 West, right before the bridge to Mann's Harbor.

The same day, Sheriff Cahoon talked to Barber's other housemate, Earl Charles Mirus Jr., the one who had reportedly left to go up north to see his girlfriend the Saturday morning Brenda vanished. Mirus rolled back into Manteo in his 1960 red MG before dawn that Wednesday morning. He went in his house and crashed. But he hadn't been asleep long before he heard someone knocking on the front door. He got up and answered it. There was his gentle boss, Quentin Bell, telling him that Brenda was missing and he needed to talk to the sheriff. Mirus, trying to take it all in, got dressed. His boss drove him to the courthouse to talk to Cahoon. A deputy led Mirus to Cahoon's office and introduced him.

The sheriff towered over Mirus, who was five feet, seven inches tall and weighed 145 pounds. But this Catholic redhead, with a habit of standing up for underdogs, would not be pushed around. When he was in grade school back in New York State and bullies were picking on an overweight boy, Mirus took to hanging out with the boy and not letting anyone mess with him. One night, while he was an undergrad at Syracuse, Mirus came upon two men beating up on a man on a dark street. Mirus walked over, saying, "Two against one, that's not fair. Let's make it two against two." The two assailants walked away.

Cahoon began by asking Mirus, "You know Brenda Holland is missing, right?"

"Yes sir, Mr. Bell just told me about it."

Cahoon told Mirus that Brenda had vanished after going home with his housemate, Danny Barber. "Tell me about yourself, where you were Friday and Saturday morning, and about your trip out of town," Cahoon told Mirus.

"Sure," Mirus said. "I'm 24 years old and working at Westvaco this summer because I'm studying for my master's degree in forestry at Duke. I'm from Clarence, in upstate New York. I left Saturday morning to visit my girlfriend in New Jersey and just got back early this morning." He continued:

> *Friday afternoon, I got off work and came home about 5 to 5:30 p.m. When I got home, there was no one there. I ate dinner there and went to a service station for a can of wax to polish my car. I did that, and worked*

on my car in front of the house until it was dark. Then I went inside and sorted some clothes and shined my shoes and went to bed about 10:30. Nobody had gotten home. I didn't see either of my housemates that night. I didn't hear anyone enter or leave the house. I got up Saturday morning at 8. I ate breakfast at home, ran some errands and left Manteo about 10:30. I drove directly to the MG dealer in Norfolk where I got some parts for my car to fix a burnt valve. I drove on to some friends' house in Asbury Park, New Jersey, stopped for a few minutes and then drove on to my girlfriend's house in Fair Haven, New Jersey, arriving after 11 p.m. Saturday. I got back here at 5:30 this morning. I knew nothing about Miss Holland being missing until my boss told me about it. I sublease rooms to Danny Barber and Rodney Brett and have only known them for about three weeks. Because of their irregular working hours, I seldom see them and don't know anything about them.

Mirus worked by day. Barber worked by night. Brett worked night and day. The sheriff thanked Mirus and asked for his girlfriend's phone number, just to verify his story. Mirus gave it to him. "Also," the sheriff asked, "will you take a polygraph test on this?"

"Sure," Mirus said.

That night, the members of *The Lost Colony* kept talking about the case. David Payne, the thirteen-year-old whom Brenda had taught to swim, said backstage, "I wish I knew who was hiding or had Brenda." Danny Barber, standing near him, said, "I do too."

"TELL ME WHO DID IT"

Evil has been wrought here, the spilling of blood, the murder of innocent ones.

—*Reverend Martin in* The Lost Colony

First we must remove the dead.

—*John White, the governor of the Roanoke colony, in* The Lost Colony

Thursday morning, July 6, 10:15 a.m. Major John A. King of the North Carolina Civil Air Patrol spotted something far below in the Albemarle Sound, gray and flat that day. He circled his small plane in for a closer look, making out what might be someone floating in the water. As he took his plane lower, he could discern that it was indeed a floater. King scanned the surrounding water, the sliver of yellow beach and the green tree line fringing it. There was no one else in the water or ashore. This was no place for recreation. He circled more and took his plane even lower, as low as he safely could. He took in a sight he'd never rub out of his mind: a body floating face-up near the shore. The corpse was bumping up against the knees of cypress trees that had been there since the American Indians ruled. King had his copilot, Captain Jack S. Howell, radio the coordinates to the Dare County Sheriff's Office in Manteo.

King's finding was a stroke of luck. The Albemarle Sound alone is 450 square miles, much less than the hundreds of square miles its connecting sounds take in where the body could have floated. Search planes were scanning those connecting waters as well. The Albemarle, like the other sounds, is shallow, just several feet deep in many spots, no more than 25 feet at its greatest depth. A body dumped in the ocean, with its far reaches and sharks, might never have been found. But sounds are more relenting of their secrets.

Sheriff Cahoon, realizing that the land search was getting nowhere, had used the governor's backing to call in Marine Corps helicopters, but they weren't spotting anything. W.W. Harvey of Manteo, the town's family practice doctor and a member of the Civil Air Patrol, had enlisted King. King was from Kinston, about 150 miles southwest of Manteo. He didn't know the Outer Banks area well. But once King's copilot called in the coordinates, deputies quickly nailed down the site. It was four miles north of the all-but-deserted fishing community of Mashoes, on the Dare County mainland. Mashoes was six miles north of Manteo, and the body was spotted at a point in the Albemarle near where the Croatan Sound flows into it. The deputies radioed their boss.

Mainland Dare County was Cahoon's world, the part of the county from which he came all those years ago. He knew every inch of that area's pinelands, water moccasin–ridden marshes and fishing camps. He knew he'd have to secure a boat, preferably one already near the site, to get to the body. Cahoon's department, covering a county that was mainly water, didn't have its own boat. But Cahoon would find one to get to that girl.

The sheriff, steering with his left hand and issuing orders to his deputies into the radio microphone in his right hand, roared out from Manteo in his cruiser, his blue lights flashing. He crossed the bridge over the Croatan Sound and then, as soon as he got off the bridge, took a hard right and raced down the desolate dirt road to Mashoes, the big car fishtailing, the pines and marshes blurring, dust in his rear-view mirror. After about five miles, the road died in Mashoes, the site of a few beat-down fishing shacks hard on the Albemarle Sound. Cahoon got out of his steaming car and walked up to the door of a vacation home of a man he knew, Jim Henson, a dentist from Greensboro.

Cahoon filled Henson in on the urgency of the situation. Henson, in his early fifties, told the sheriff he'd be glad to help. As Henson prepared his boat, loading in a canvass tarp, Cahoon radioed his dispatcher to have the North Carolina Highway Patrol, which often took crime scene photos, to send in a trooper. He also told the dispatcher to alert local photographer Aycock Brown.

Major King circled the site in his plane, keeping an eye on the body and his sinking gas gauge. Dr. Henson was soon ferrying the sheriff toward the spot. Henson sat in the stern of the twenty-foot boat, working its small outboard motor, leaving a white plume in the gray water, the gas smell acrid in the humid air. Cahoon sat in the bow, watching the water closely. He spotted the body in the shallows by the shore and yelled to Henson. The dentist brought the boat in close. Major King flew off.

The sheriff climbed out of the boat, the water rising past the top of his leather boots, up to the knees of his khakis. Using the tarp, he and the dentist pulled the body into the boat. Cahoon had seen a lot of corpses, but this one must have been especially hard. The body was markedly bloated and decomposed. It bore numerous lacerations and bruises, including on the face, as well as some type of marks across the neck. Only a few strands of blond hair remained. The tip of the tongue was visible between clenched teeth. A maroon skirt clung to the body. The lower two-thirds of the skirt were turned inside out and pulled up to the level of the waist. On the torso were a silver necklace and some type of sleeveless garment with a leopard-skin design. There was no blouse nor shoes. The smell, exacerbated by the July heat, was overpowering.

The sheriff had studied Brenda's photo from *The Lost Colony* program. The decomposed body bore but scant resemblance to her. But he knew from descriptions of the last clothes she wore, given by her roommate, that this was Brenda.

Cahoon covered the body with the tarp and bid Henson to take them the short distance back to Mashoes. Henson soon pulled up at the small dock there. Cahoon climbed out of the boat and walked over to his patrol car. He radioed his dispatcher, telling him to send Dr. Harvey out and to have Twiford's Funeral Home in Manteo send a hearse and a body bag. "Call the medical examiner's office and tell them we'll be sending them, late this afternoon, a body for autopsy ASAP." The sheriff added, "And have a deputy bring Danny Barber out here too."

As Cahoon waited, he had Dr. Henson take a look at the corpse's teeth. The dentist found some of them to be loose. Somebody probably hit her in the mouth, he said. The state trooper shot photos of the corpse.

The black hearse, a 1964 Cadillac, arrived. The driver, along with some of the other men, put the corpse in the back of the hearse. Dr. Harvey arrived and took a perfunctory look at the body. He noted that it had probably been in the water for several days. He left further examination and findings to the pathologist. Aycock Brown also drove up in his big Chevy with the license plate that bore his first name. He snapped photos of the body.

A deputy drove Barber in. He got out of the car and met Cahoon under the sun. They stared at each other, seagulls cackling overhead. Barber, bearded and wearing glasses, had on a striped fisherman's shirt tucked into blue jeans. Cahoon, clean-shaven, wore khakis, a white open-collar shirt with sleeves folded casually just above his wrists and a straw beach hat with a small brim and a striped band. He had a pen and small notepad in the pocket over his heart, ready to record Barber's words. Thousands of cicadas buzzed from the pines. The men nearby smoked, wiped sweat off their brows and took it in—this showdown between the sheriff and the college boy some of them were sure had offed that girl and thought he could get away with it, figuring the sheriff and the rest of them were just a bunch of hicks.

Cahoon, always the political animal, felt their stares and Aycock Brown's camera lens. The sheriff led Barber over to the hearse, its tailgate open, the body clearly visible. He wanted Barber to identify her. Brenda's parents were in Manteo and could have been driven in for the identification. But Cahoon wanted Barber to do it in hopes of breaking him, of driving a confession out of him.

"Can you identify her, Danny?" the sheriff asked. He stood close, looming over the chorus singer. Barber took a look, walked a few feet away and then returned. "That's Brenda," he told the sheriff. Cahoon wondered how he could know that, given the massive decomposition and what might have been Barber's booze-hazed memory of what she was wearing. As Cahoon kept that question to himself, Barber said something else to him. He knew it was Brenda because of the necklace on the body. It was the one she was given from her beauty pageant back home last year.

Checkmate. The sheriff had thought he had something on Barber. The boy was smart. Cahoon was not done with him. This was going to be a long game. "You're free to go," the sheriff told Barber. Barber climbed into the deputy's car for the ride back to Manteo.

Cahoon was losing control of the crime scene. In taking more photos, Aycock Brown removed Brenda's necklace, tearing badly decomposed skin away with it. He washed it off in the water by the nearby dock, a good man meaning well but not a lawman, and took photos of the necklace. Then he handed the jewelry to the sheriff.

At about 2:00 p.m., Cahoon nodded at the hearse driver. The driver zipped up the body bag, slammed the tailgate, started up the big V-8 and set out for the Norfolk office of the Virginia State Medical Examiner. The autopsy would be done there because it was the closest morgue with the best pathologists. North Carolina lacked a statewide medical examiner's office.

The driver was alone with Brenda's body. The black hearse rolled across the William B. Umstead bridge over the Croatan Sound and through Manteo, the town Brenda had come to love. The hearse rolled through Nags Head, past the sand mountain, Jockey's Ridge, that Brenda had marveled at and climbed. The car cruised on, north toward Norfolk. The previous Friday night, Brenda had made plans with two fellow members of the *Lost Colony* crew to visit that port city. That was just six days past.

After the hearse pulled away, Sheriff Cahoon drove from Mashoes to Dick and Cora Gray Twiford's house in Manteo, where Brenda's parents had been spending their daytime hours. The Hollands met the sheriff in the Twifords' living room. He took off his hat and met the gaze of the Hollands. "She's gone," he told them in his workaday voice. "They just found her body in the sound."

He handed Brenda's necklace to her father. "It was her most cherished possession," Shotgun Holland told the sheriff. "All I want you to do is tell me who did it." The sheriff nodded. He didn't want Shotgun Holland to know that he already suspected Barber. Cahoon did not want another killing.

Brenda's treasured necklace, pictured here in 2018, was found on her corpse. *Courtesy Kim Holland Thorn.*

Molly Black, Brenda's roommate, was standing nearby. Cahoon, who'd met her earlier in the week when he had her describe the last clothes Brenda was wearing, now needed more. He asked her for details on the blouse Brenda was wearing the night she vanished. The sheriff was troubled by the fact that the blouse had been missing from the body. He knew that its absence could figure in the case. Black described the garment: three-quarter-inch sleeves with deep red, deep pink, orange and a bit of brown and green colors all splashed together. The blouse buttoned up the front, Black said, and had a small collar. Then Black saw the necklace Shotgun Holland held and recognized it as Brenda's. She burst into tears. A friend led her away. The tension was twisting her. The day before, she'd lashed out at Brenda's father over some words he'd said about what he'd do with anyone who had hurt his daughter.

Brenda's necklace stayed with Shotgun Holland from that Thursday on.

Cahoon collected other evidence at Brenda's rooming house that day: the clothes she had been wearing earlier the previous Friday, before she changed into the clothes she wore that night, and strands of her hair, gently gathered by her mother from a plastic curler she had used.

Gerri Holland telephoned her daughter Ann, up in the mountains, with the bad news. Ann and her husband, Vernon Earley, had been looking after Kim and Little Charles. Ann and Vernon had been fielding calls all week from worried friends and family. Loved ones streamed through the house with covered dishes of fried chicken, pimento cheese sandwiches, chicken salad, potato salad, macaroni and cheese and banana pudding—southern comfort food. They brought the food and hugs and hope that week. Now the hope was gone. As Ann and her mother finished the hardest talk they ever had, including plans for Brenda's funeral, Ann tried to stop crying. She hung up and hugged her husband. He knew before she said the words: Brenda had been killed. She filled him in on the part about Brenda's body being found in the sound and the few other details Cahoon and company had relayed through Gerri. Then Ann and Vernon called Little Charles and Kim into their bedroom.

Vernon told them, "I have something very important to tell you. Your sister Brenda is never coming home because someone killed her." Ann and her husband cried, and so did Little Charles, who was twelve. Kim, who was nine, was confused and sad because everyone was crying, so she cried too.

Little Charles was broken but not surprised. He'd had a bad feeling about Manteo from the time Brenda said she was going there for the summer. He envisioned her walking barefoot on the beach, finding sand dollars, starfish and big conch shells, and thought about the seashell collection she had sent him. He thought about the previous December, when Brenda had arrived home on Christmas Eve, disappointed because the family had already cut a Christmas tree from Holland Mountain and had it up in their living room. She had wanted to be part of the tree search and cutting. Little Charles put on his coat and told Brenda to as well. They walked back up Holland Mountain and cut another tree, one just for Brenda, a tree that they agreed was perfect. They pulled the tree down the mountain and then paused to rest in a field near their house. Darkness was falling and so was light snow. Little Charles and Brenda sat down in the field, stared up at the winter sky and started talking about old times growing up, Brenda's dreams and her dreams for him. They chatted on and on for more than an hour, watching the stars come out. Finally, they rose, dragged their tree home and persuaded the family to take down the old one and replace it with theirs. Brenda just beamed—big-eyed, loving, happy.

IN MANTEO BY LATE that Thursday afternoon, the main conduit of information, as it had always been on the island, was word of mouth. The locals read the *Coastland Times*, listened to the area radio stations and watched the scratchy reception of the TV news out of Norfolk, Virginia, but more than anything else, they listened to one another. Word that Brenda's body had been found was talked about in shops, restaurants, bars, the post office, on the sidewalks, on boats and on the docks. The islanders chatted about it in between ringing up sales on cash registers, serving food and drinks, sorting mail and cleaning fish. It was the hot topic in the little houses of Goat Town and California and in the big houses of Mother Vineyard.

The news resonated throughout the local grapevine. They couldn't stop talking about the crime. "Did you hear what they said she looked like?…She was beautiful, but when they pulled her out of the sound, oh my God…. Somebody's got to catch that killer….This sort of thing just can't be allowed to happen on our island."

It wasn't just *the* death. It was *this* death. Death in the water had long been grimly accepted on the island. The week Brenda vanished, two tourists died in the surf over on the beach, joining a long line of thousands of other tourists of all ages who'd drowned on the beach, as well as thousands of others just offshore in the Graveyard of the Atlantic—tattooed sailors the sea had sucked in and so many others, howls in the raging night of the sea sometimes within sight of the lights of land, falling victim to everything from hurricanes to lightning strikes to Germans subs in both world wars.

Many of the locals went to the sea in fishing trawlers, knowing that, just as with their ancestors and brothers, they could die too, maybe even close to home, their ravaged bodies bobbing in the sea or sounds with crabs clawing and sharks nipping. They were some of the most rugged fishermen in the world, renowned not just for navigating their own treacherous waters but also for going far beyond, into the Grand Banks off Newfoundland and other hell spots. Outer Bankers had been heroes on fishing boats and with the Life-Saving Service and its successor, the Coast Guard, charging out into mountainous waves toward screaming victims clinging to sinking ships, sometimes drowning in the process. The service's unofficial motto was "You have to go out, but you don't have to come back." Just a little more than two decades before, islanders had dealt with casualties of German submarines, burned bodies in flaming oil-soaked waters.

The islanders carried on the tradition in their boats, looking out for one another. They knew the stories of tragedy from their mothers and fathers. They knew that helping a fellow boat crew in peril was much more than an obligation. It was a sacred trust of their watery way, just as they helped one another out on land in recovering from hurricanes. They held their sheriff up to their standards.

They drank their coffee and beer as they talked about Brenda. They stood on the docks, smoking, tossing their butts in the water and watching them drift. They knew what the cost of their watery way could be. They knew that they could lose their houses and lives to hurricanes and floods and that tourists, even toddler tourists, were going to drown. It wasn't pretty, but there it was—nature, the cost of the game. That was God's business.

What happened to Brenda was different. It touched the hardest-hearted fishermen and made even the most god-fearing ones question their Lord. Nature hadn't gotten her, but man's evil had, this innocent they should have protected. Somebody was going to pay. The pressure was on Cahoon. At the Pioneer Theater in Manteo, *The Alamo*, starring John Wayne as the outgunned Davy Crockett, would start Saturday. Cahoon did have some help: the SBI would soon authorize its five agents already arriving on the scene to stay on site through the summer or the solution of the case, whichever came first. The sheriff would need that aid. He'd worked only a few murder cases in his county, just shootings and stabbings where the killer was readily apparent and charged.

Cahoon told a local reporter that he had no idea how Brenda had died and would leave that question to the pathologist. "This is no matter for an amateur to guess at," he said. It's possible that her body was dumped into the Croatan Sound from the Umstead Bridge, he said, and then drifted north to the point where it was found, in the mouth of the Albemarle Sound. Tide tables would support that theory. The body would have initially sank and then slowly risen.

The William B. Umstead Bridge, from Roanoke Island to the mainland, from which investigators theorized Brenda's body was thrown. *Photo by the author.*

Some people speculated that Brenda might have taken her own life. Shotgun Holland told Cahoon, "Sheriff, no matter what they tell you, she didn't commit suicide."

Danny Barber was mostly silent. He did tell the *Virginian-Pilot* newspaper of Norfolk early Thursday, before Brenda's body was found, that Brenda was "a wonderful girl" and that he was angered by news stories that indicated otherwise. By then, newspaper writers had reported that Brenda had gone back to Barber's house and then his room right before she vanished. The *Pilot* reported Friday that Barber had agreed Thursday to let one of its reporters interview him about Brenda but canceled the interview after her body was found, saying he didn't feel like it. "He looked tired and strained," the paper reported. "Friends said he was grieved by Miss Holland's death."

Backstage at *The Lost Colony* Thursday night, Barber again declined to talk about Brenda's death. "I've been through a hell of a lot this week," he told a reporter for the *Charlotte Observer*.

By then, Brenda's corpse was on a pathologist's slab in Norfolk. On Friday, the pathologist, Heinz Karnitschnig, phoned Cahoon with the preliminary cause of death: ligature strangulation. And Brenda may have been raped.

Part II

THE INVESTIGATION

MANTEO, NORTH CAROLINA
JULY 1967–FEBRUARY 1971

"If There Is Any Justice"

As the sun rose high over the sea on Friday, July 7, Sheriff Cahoon pulled his cruiser up to the Ocean House, the motel he partially owned in Kill Devil Hills. It was a sturdy brick affair with a fine outdoor pool in its center, a favorite of southeastern Virginians and northeastern North Carolinians. The five SBI agents on the case were already working from there.

The sheriff walked into the motel office, poured himself a cup of coffee and bid good morning to Annie Mae Midgett, his friend who ran the front desk. The sheriff was headed to Norfolk to talk to the pathologist about Brenda's autopsy. SBI agent Lenny Wise, Cahoon's longtime friend and fellow native of mainland Dare County, was going with him. Midgett, a silver-haired widow as warm as an apple pie, told the sheriff she'd ring Wise's room. On the front desk counter was that day's edition of the *Coastland Times*, full of front-page news on the discovery of Brenda's body.

A little more than an hour later, Cahoon and Wise were sitting in the office of Dr. Heinz Karnitschnig, the chief pathologist for the Norfolk office of the Virginia State Medical Examiner. The autopsy had taken place from 4:30 p.m. to 6:45 p.m. the day before. Brenda should have been headed for work around that time. Others in Manteo and over on the beach that holiday week were settling on their porches for cocktails and making dinner plans—tanned women in Lilly Pulitzer dresses with hair held tight by Final Net hairspray, men in Bermuda shorts with faces red, listening to record players from inside blaring Sinatra's *Summer Wind* and other beach classics. But by Friday morning, Brenda's parents were numb in their Ford

The finding of Brenda's corpse carried the front page of the July 7, 1967 issue of the *Coastland Times*. *Author's personal collection.*

Sunliner—Shotgun driving, smoking and raving, Gerri mostly silent, into the longest ride of their lives, back to the Smoky Mountains to plan a funeral they never saw coming. An ambulance was on a parallel track, driving their daughter's body from the pathologist's office to Canton.

Cahoon told the pathologist to tell him and Wise about his findings on Brenda's death. Karnitschnig was a short, bearded man with a heavy head of hair, brown with streaks of blond. He was thirty-seven, a rising star in his field and younger than the lawmen. He'd grown up in Austria during World War II. His father, a lawyer, was drafted into Hitler's army and then went missing in action. Karnitschnig was pressed into the Hitler Youth movement, but he couldn't stand the dictator. As a young teenager during the war, Karnitschnig had helped drag bodies out of buildings bombed by the Allies.

During the American occupation after the war, Karnitschnig served as a translator for American troops. They paid him with cigarettes, starting him on a long habit. His father found his way back to the family after the war. He'd been held as a prisoner of war in Yugoslavia.

The son was educated in his native country and did residencies in Scotland and Canada before arriving in Virginia. He could be charming and compassionate but also arrogant and short-tempered. He didn't suffer fools lightly. He lit up a cigarette and began, in his Austrian accent, to tell the lawmen about the autopsy, hitting the most important points first. Wise took these notes:

> *The cause of death is ligature strangulation. The neck shows a completely circumferential and horizontal constriction measuring between three-eighths inch and one-half-inch in width and between one-fourth inch and three-eighths inch in depth over the right side of the back of the neck. There are two distinct corrugated ligature imprints one-quarter inch in width and showing a ropelike, crisscross pattern. They measure three inches in length each, and meet in the midline and diverge.*
>
> *There are lacerations of the hymen and vagina. The labia majora are swollen and are dark purple. The external orifice of the urethra shows an irregular laceration at 7 o'clock measuring one-eighth of an inch in length. The annular hymen shows a radial tear at 8 o'clock. This measures one-quarter inch in length and is bordered by intensely congested hymenal tissues. The vagina in its upper one-third between 7 and 8 o'clock shows a longitudinal laceration measuring three-fourths inch in length and gaping one-eighth inches.*

> *There are contusions of the face, scalp, left arm, left chest wall, left thigh and left ankle. The body is markedly decomposed. The scalp hair is largely absent due to post-mortem decomposition. A few strands of scalp hair are light blond. The soft tissue of the nose is largely absent. The entire body is markedly bloated and shows generalized skin slipping.*
>
> *The body was dressed in a maroon skirt which was quite tight. It was buttoned and completely zipped up. The lower two-thirds of the skirt were turned inside out and pulled up to the level of the waist. The torso was covered with a tight-fitting costume showing a leopard-skin pattern. It has black shoulder straps. After the skirt and costume was cut away, the body was found to be further dressed in a matching pair of panties and a bra showing a blue and yellow flowery pattern.*

The autopsy raised more questions than it answered. If Brenda had been sexually assaulted or raped, how come her underclothes, including the teddy, and her skirt were still on? It didn't make sense that, if her killer had raped her, he would have had the time or dexterity to put her clothing back on. Cahoon would soon use that reasoning to publicly discount the pathologist's conclusion that Brenda may have been raped. "Nobody who raped her would bother to dress her again," he would tell a reporter.

Could she have been sexually assaulted days before she was killed?

Cahoon and Agent Wise collected Brenda's clothes from the pathologist to send to the Federal Bureau of Investigation (FBI) for testing. Back in Manteo that week, before the clothes were sent off, Manteo police chief C.C. Duvall handed them, in a plastic bag, to a teenage friend of his to wash. He told her they were the clothes Brenda Holland had been wearing. The girl was seventeen and married. Like everybody else on the island, she knew who Brenda was. The clothes, after all that time in the sound, were just stinking up the sheriff's office, Duvall told her.

Duvall did not share office space with the sheriff. Duvall didn't have jurisdiction in the case, since the body had been found just outside the Manteo town limits, in the county. But Duvall and the sheriff were friends, and Duvall probably had the clothes washed at Cahoon's request and hadn't thought about the ramifications. Duvall, a lanky thirty-year-old army vet and graduate of Beaufort County Community College, was from a good family in Manteo. He was well liked.

The teenager who washed the clothes at a downtown Manteo laundromat would say years later, "I didn't think anything of it. I was 17. The clothes were in a plastic bag, tied up to keep the smell in. I opened the bag and held it over the washing machine and dumped them in. I was probably gagging, because I was pregnant." After the washing was finished, she put the clothes in a dryer until they were done and then folded them and gave them back to Chief Duvall.

There was nothing nefarious about it, she said. She was sure of the timing, she said, because her baby, her first, was born in mid-July 1967, days after the body was found.

As Sheriff Cahoon and the SBI agents began their investigation, the Hollands, up in Canton, bid farewell to their daughter. They received family and friends at the Wells Funeral Home on the night of Saturday, July 8, which would have been Brenda's twentieth birthday. The next afternoon at 4:00 p.m., Reverends Fred Fore and Edwin Young held the funeral at the Hollands' church, Ridgeway Baptist, on the Old Asheville Highway east of Canton. The Hollands lived in a two-story brick home about three miles from the church. A limousine from the funeral home picked up the family at their homeplace, with Shotgun and Gerri leading the way to the car, followed by Ann and Vernon and their girls and Little Charles and Kim. As they approached the brick church, shadowed by a mountain, they took in a long line of cars and pickup trucks parked by the road, a testament to the high regard for Brenda.

A light rain was falling. Brenda never liked rain. There was an overflow crowd in the chapel, including a couple of Brenda's friends from Manteo. There was a white casket draped with flowers at the front. Because of the condition of Brenda's body, the coffin was closed. Near it was a pedestal with a framed photo on it of Brenda from a few years ago when her hair was brown. She smiled out at the crowd. Shotgun and Gerri sat near the coffin on a front pew with their surviving children. Shotgun, uncomfortable as always in his Sunday best, was stone-faced, as was his son. Gerri and Ann dabbed at tears. Kim just looked numb, confused about what it all meant.

Reverend Young, a favorite of Brenda's, said that the rain outside was angels crying for her. He acknowledged the eternal question of why bad things happen to good people. Satan, he said, is awfully strong. He described Brenda as "a fine Christian girl" who had nightly brought carloads of her fellow students from Campbell College to a revival he conducted that spring in the town of Lillington, near the school. He talked

Brenda's funeral was held outside her hometown of Canton, North Carolina. *Courtesy Kim Holland Thorn.*

about everlasting life in heaven. His words were cold comfort to some in Brenda's family. She was gone. She was not coming back. Her killer was still out there somewhere.

The grim-faced pallbearers carried Brenda's casket out to the family's spot in the cemetery. Just a few years before, the graveyard had been a vacant hill. Brenda had played there as a child. As church leaders mapped the cemetery, Shotgun and Gerri purchased plots, figuring their children would bury them there.

As a preacher said final words before Brenda's coffin was lowered, the rain stopped. On Brenda's gravestone of cherrystone were these words: "Always thinking of others, she walked in beauty and grace." Gerri, inspired by classic poetry, had ordered the phrase.

At the same time that Sunday afternoon, Brenda's island friends were saying their goodbyes at Manteo Baptist Church, an imposing brick building with white columns on U.S. 64. About one hundred members of the *Colony* company filed into the sanctuary and took their seats on hard pews. They'd donned the only nice dresses and sports jackets they'd brought to the coast. Some were used to church. Others were not. Some might have been atheists. The year before, *Time* magazine had featured a cover story asking, in big red letters against a black background, "Is God Dead?"

The actors and actresses in the Manteo church were used to trying on new identities, but this was one role they knew nothing about. Most of them were young. They'd experienced the demise of grandparents and maybe parents, but few contemporaries, especially ones slain. The women, and some of the men, cried. They reached out hands to one another. Some of them scanned the pews in front and behind them, noting who was there and who was not. They whispered to each other that Danny Barber was not in their midst. Several locals surrounded them, offering the best sympathetic looks they could, as lost as the *Colony* crew.

They all watched as the church pastor in his red robe, W.S. Brown, took his place, standing at the altar splashed with white gladiolus and lavender dahlias. Death after long illness or after a long and useful life is sometimes a blessing, he said, "but when it comes to youth with such suddenness, it leaves us stunned and bewildered. We honor one whose life was cut short. And, as we do so, we remember the words of Christ, who said, 'Fear not them which kill the body, but are not able to kill the soul, but rather fear him who is able to destroy both body and soul.'"

Brown read from the Psalms and the Gospel of John. Then he touched on justice—God's justice. Of the hundreds of letters that the Hollands were starting to receive, one friend wrote, "We hear and read about things like this happening to someone else, but we never think it can happen to us. If there is any justice in this world or the next, and I believe there is, whoever did this won't go unpunished."

Reverend Brown carried on that theme: "We are all under God's care. He knows all that we do. He will bring to light the hidden works of darkness."

As the service went on, the SBI agents were having a sit-down with Danny Barber at the sheriff's office, their own attempt to bring that light.

SBI AGENT LENNY WISE had stopped by Barber's house that morning, telling Barber that he and the other agents wanted to interview him. Barber reluctantly agreed and rode downtown with Wise. In the sheriff's office at the courthouse, Wise and Barber sat down in an interview room and were joined by Agents Charlie Ray, Jack Thomas and Dan Gilbert. It was four on one. For hours, the agents pressed Barber with all they had, as hard as they could, hoping to get a confession.

Barber had never felt so scared, alone, vulnerable and helpless. He was an outsider on an island of insiders. He knew the county jail was adjacent to the courthouse. He knew Central Prison was in Raleigh. He knew what happened to nice boys like him in there. And he knew the gas chamber was in that prison.

The agents started out by asking Barber to tell them about himself. He said he was from a family of four in Goldsboro. His father was dead, and his mother was a seamstress for a local department store. He was a student at Carolina, he said, and had spent three years in the U.S. Army band, 1961 through 1964, and was honorably discharged. Barber was proud of that service at a time when many conservative law enforcement officers were clashing with protesters of the Vietnam War.

His army service didn't win any points with the agents. Tell us about your criminal record, one of them asked him. The lawmen had already pulled Barber's sheet. But they wanted to know what he'd volunteer about it. "My only criminal record is for speeding in 1965," Barber said. "I was picked up in Chapel Hill, arrested on a peeping tom charge, but that was dismissed."

Tell us about your date with Brenda, one of the agents asked. Barber gave his statement:

> On Friday night, June 30, Brenda and I were both at The Lost Colony. I did my regular performance as a singer that night, then Brenda and I left about 11:30. We went to the Drafty Tavern and had one beer before last call. Charlie Smith, also a company member, and I shot pool and his wife and Brenda talked. We stayed there while the man cleaned up the bar and left about 12:30 to 12:45 a.m. We went to the beach, to Jennette's Pier, and watched people shark fishing. We ran into [Houston Rob Waters] and talked to him for quite some time. Brenda told me she knew him because he dated her roommate. We stayed at the pier until about 1:30 and we left and went up the beach to Jockey's Ridge. We walked up the ridge a short distance and then left. We came back to Manteo, to my house, getting there about 2 to 2:15 a.m. Both my housemates' cars were there. We went into the living room and I could hear one of my housemates, Rodney Brett, in his bedroom.
>
> Brenda sat down in the living room and I went into the kitchen, got two beers, and came back in the living room. Realizing we might be making too much noise and keeping Rodney awake, we decided to go

upstairs to my bedroom. We laid down on the bed and started to read a Playboy magazine. I made out with Brenda but did not have sex with her. We liked each other very much and talked freely to each other about her problems or any other matter.

I started reading some excerpts from Playboy to her and then I passed her the magazine and she started reading some of it to me. That's when I fell asleep. I don't know when she left or how.

On Saturday night when I got to work for that night's performance, I didn't know Brenda was missing. But when I got to the theater, Renie Rains, Brenda's boss, came up and asked me where Brenda was. She told me Brenda hadn't come to work. Renie and I then went and told John Fox, the manager of the show, and he called Sheriff Cahoon and told him about Brenda being missing.

I had dated Brenda three times, and had her over, but the night she disappeared was the only night she had ever been upstairs to my room. We talked about a date she had with [Rob Breeze], *a local guy, and about him going to bed with her, about the rough treatment. It was very repulsive and it had changed her outlook on life.*

In response to questioning about what Brenda had on her during her date with him, Barber accurately described the clothing in which her body had been found. But he said she'd also been wearing a blouse. The agents pressed him: What happened to the blouse? Barber maintained that he didn't know, that she'd had it on in his room.

The agents moved on Barber even harder, trying to get a confession. He wasn't budging. Finally, after several hours that Sunday, they told him that he was free to go. After Barber left, the agents hashed out his statement. They might have been bothered by his assertion that he had Brenda come up to his bedroom so they wouldn't disturb Brett. They might have figured that was his excuse, but the real point was to get her upstairs and have sex. Maybe, upstairs, she tried to stop him and he got mad and strangled her. Maybe he hadn't meant to kill her. Maybe he just lost control. Then, he somehow got Brenda's body out of the house and into his car, drove to the bridge and dumped it.

There was something just too smooth about Barber that bothered the agents. He had been less than honest at one point in the interview and in the days before. In talking about the conversations about Brenda at *The Lost Colony* on Saturday, July 1, Barber had left out the fact he'd initially said he took Brenda back to her boardinghouse, a change in his story that continued to plague him. And contrary to other witnesses, he'd claimed he had played an active role in telling Fox that Brenda was missing.

The agents decided to keep Barber in their sights and to investigate what he said Brenda had told him about her rough date with Rob Breeze. If Barber was right, that might explain the bruising and tearing that led the pathologist to say she might have been raped.

The agents also decided to take another run at Barber's housemate Rodney Brett. They wanted to see if he had more on Barber. And they believed Brett was a suspect as well—his car had been misfiring badly, and he had gone to Virginia on July 11 and 12 to see about trading it for another car. This was important, because Robert Midgett—who lived down the street from Barber, Brett and Mirus and had described the "ungodly scream" about 3:00 a.m. on the July 1 predawn morning Brenda vanished—said that he heard a car having trouble about the same time. Brett was also struggling with being gay ("homosexual" in the 1967 vernacular). He'd come to the Outer Banks searching for a place where he could belong.

Investigators hit on a theory that because Brett was gay, he may have hated women and jumped Brenda after she left the house he shared with Barber and Mirus. Homophobia was a theme in the investigation, as common as one of those brackish canals by U.S. 64 in mainland Dare County. Investigators routinely asked Barber and other suspects if they had homosexual tendencies, as if that might figure in homicidal tendencies. A judge in Williamston, a small town a few hours' drive west from Manteo on 64, confidentially told investigators about "a group of homosexuals" in his town who partied at the beach and might be connected to Brenda's slaying. His tip proved groundless.

But against that backdrop, the SBI agents sat down with Rodney Brett on Friday, July 14, at his workplace, the Carolinian Hotel in Nags Head. Brett was twenty-nine. He was living at the Carolinian, having moved out of the house he had shared with Barber and Earl Mirus. He was nervous and did not want to stay there any longer, as he had told Sheriff Cahoon on July 2. Brett had not elaborated, but the agents couldn't help but wonder about his move.

SBI agents Charlie Ray and Dan Gilbert followed up on Cahoon's interview and pushed further. Gilbert began by advising Brett of his Miranda rights, a practice mandated by a Supreme Court decision just a year before. Suspects presumed to be in custody had to be warned of their rights.

Gilbert read the warning to Brett: "You have the right to remain silent. Anything you say can and will be used against you in a court of law. You have the right to an attorney. If you cannot afford an attorney, one will be provided for you. Do you understand these rights?"

"I do," Brett said. He told the agents that he was from Franklin, Virginia, a paper mill town in rural Tidewater, a drive of about two hours west of the beach. He had attended Chowan College in nearby Murfreesboro for a year, and he was in the U.S. Navy for about three and a half years. He began with the basic details he'd told the sheriff about returning home the night Brenda vanished. As he continued, he elaborated on his earlier statement:

After I got in bed and was half-asleep, I heard someone come in the front door. I assumed it was Danny. I did not hear any other footsteps to indicate that there were two people. Whoever it was went straight to the bathroom and upstairs, he didn't go into the kitchen. After I heard the footsteps going up the stairs, a few minutes later, I heard a girl whisper, about twice. At that time, the bed began to squeak with a steady regularity like they were having sex. A short while later, I fell asleep. Later on, I heard the cat that hangs around the house crawling up the screen door and I heard someone coming real quietly down the stairway. Whoever it was opened the screen door very cautiously and left. I did not hear a car leave the yard. I did not hear any other sounds in the front yard and went back to sleep. I got up the next morning and went to work about 7:45 a.m. I didn't notice anything unusual about the front room or any other part of the house. I didn't go upstairs. When I left for work, Danny's car was in the front yard and I think Earl's was, too.

At 9:30 p.m. Saturday, the next night, Danny Barber called me at The Carolinian and said, "You didn't know this, but I brought a girl home last night and now she is missing." I told him, "I did know because I heard you upstairs." Danny said, "Did you see anyone in the living room before you left this morning?" I told him I did not see anyone in the living room.

About 1 a.m. Sunday morning, I got home and Danny Barber came in just a little later and told me about bringing the girl home the night before. I told him I heard them upstairs. Danny said they came in and had a beer from the kitchen. I told him I did not hear them go to the kitchen. Danny said, "You won't believe this, but I did not take her to bed." I told Danny I did not believe it, and he got mad and went to his room.

Agents Ray and Gilbert questioned Brett about leaving the Nags Head area earlier that week, on Tuesday and Wednesday. Brett replied:

I went to Franklin to visit my family. After I got there, I talked to my mother about trading my 1960 black Falcon, which had 79,000 to 80,000 miles on it. My brother-in-law, who is a used-car dealer, gave me a good deal and, since my old car was wearing out, I thought I should trade it. The Falcon sounded like it was going to blow up and was skipping badly. The muffler was worn out, and roaring, and numerous other things were wrong with the car. When I got back to The Carolinian, my boss lady jumped on me and said I did not have common sense, leaving the area so shortly after Brenda Holland was killed. I told her that was my business, and she said she would call the sheriff and explain to him why I left. But later, I asked her if she had called the sheriff and she said she did not.

My mother called me and told me that the police in Franklin had searched my car at my brother-in-law's used car lot. Earl Mirus told me yesterday that he heard that I gone out to The Lost Colony and dug a grave, and that people were talking about me and suspecting me of killing Brenda Holland. Earl told me about his interview with the investigating agents.

I have known Earl since I rented the room about a month before the crime occurred. He's a very nice, quiet, intelligent person. I've never seen him drunk.

I've often been drunk. Two years ago on the Outer Banks, I tried to commit suicide, after a homosexual relationship. I slashed both my wrists and called a Methodist minister by the name of Hank Wilkerson. He came to my home and, along with the policeman, gave me emergency aid and I recovered from my wounds. Wilkerson and I became good friends and visited together often. He is a fine man and has done me a lot of good, and since being acquainted with him, I have not had any homosexual relationships. Due to him, I got a job at The Carolinian.

I never lose my memory while drinking, except when I pass out. I know I didn't do anything Friday night or Saturday morning, July 1. I had met Brenda Holland at a party at my house and thought she was a very nice girl, level-headed and respectable. She was quiet and reserved. I had a lot of respect for the girl.

We had a lot of parties at my house when I was living with Danny Barber and Earl Mirus. I have, on at least one occasion, insulted some of the guests because of their crude manners.

I don't know anything about the death of Brenda Joyce Holland, and I have not withheld any information in regard to this crime.

Agents Ray and Gilbert finished up and left the Carolinian. The statement had given them much to think about. Brett had said his car had been "skipping badly." Could that have been the backfiring Robert Midgett heard during the early morning hours in which Brenda vanished?

If Brett was telling the truth about what Barber had told him, Barber didn't know what happened to Brenda and had been trying to find out by asking Brett if he had seen anyone in the living room before he left for work. Or Barber was trying to mask his actions.

Regarding Brett's statement about a grave, a freshly dug, grave-sized depression had been found near the *Lost Colony* grounds. Bobby Long, a teenager who played a colonist, and a friend had come across it the week before just off the highway, between the entrance to the theater grounds and the bridge to the mainland. That was during the search for Brenda. Long and his friend had struck off on their own and were walking by the road when they noticed tire tracks leading into woods of pine. They followed the tracks through tall grass. Several feet into the woods, they spotted the depression. It was about five feet long, four inches deep and thirty inches wide. It seemed to have been dug by hand. To the boys, it appeared to be a shallow grave. They found a receipt for gas lying on the ground near it. Long recognized the signature on the receipt as "Brett," whom he knew was one of Barber's housemates. The boys reported their finding to a law enforcement officer and gave him the receipt. Investigators never told the boys what they did with the receipt, nor did they definitively tie it to Rodney Brett. But word of the discovery leaked, causing the rumor that Brett dug a grave. For his part, Brett was vehement that he was not involved in the killing. When he'd visited his mother, he told her that he'd had nothing to do with Brenda's death and didn't know who killed her.

For the investigators, Brett and Barber were two of several suspects developing in the case.

PACKING A PISTOL AND TEAR GAS

Two weeks ago, I moved out of Mrs. Twiford's to a house with some girls in the show. We have such a lovely house and everything is fixed up beautifully. We keep everything locked up and a pistol in the bedroom upstairs. I carry a tear-gas gun with me.

—July 30, 1967 letter from Brenda's roommate, Molly Black, to Brenda's parents

By late July 1967, with no arrests in Brenda's slaying, Roanoke Island and the nearby beach towns were on guard. Media coverage remained heavy. A few civilians saw, on Aycock Brown's desk in his cluttered office in downtown Manteo, the photos he shot of the corpse. Those viewers told friends about the shocking sepia images, and those friends told other friends. Much was lost in the telling, but a central truth remained: A killer had taken an innocent on the island.

The fear and tension soon after Brenda's body was found produced numerous tips. One concerned a resident of Mother Vineyard. David Edward Whaley, who was nineteen, had recently moved into his grandfather's soundfront home there. The grandfather, Ken Whitney, a Massachusetts native, had for four years been the rector of St. Andrew's By the Sea in Nags Head. The Episcopal church, on the west side of the Beach Road, catered to the wealthy families from the cottages of the Unpainted Aristocracy that surrounded it. David Whaley along with his mother, Nancy, and brother,

Jonathan, had lived in Durham, near the state capital of Raleigh. They moved into the Manteo home of Nancy's father, Reverend Whitney, after she and her husband divorced.

On Sunday, July 16, Sheriff Cahoon told Agent Ray to check out Whaley, a slim six-footer with brown hair and blue eyes. He was a smart preppy with an angular face, big ears, a soft smile and a Durham juvenile record of minor crimes. Sources told Cahoon that Whaley had been reported riding around downtown Manteo and on Barber's road around the time Brenda vanished, about 3:00 a.m. on July 1. He hadn't been seen riding around downtown since Brenda vanished. That was unusual, because he usually cruised the area late at night. He had worked at the Carolinian as a waiter and at a Manteo bank as a cashier and was fired from both jobs. Whaley, who'd dropped out of East Carolina University in Greenville, was considered unpredictable when he drank. And he drank quite a bit. On Sundays, as the white-robed Reverend Whitney stood at his Nags Head altar and read from his worn copy of the *Book of Common Prayer*, his grandson David was not seated among the faithful.

One of the sources talking about Whaley was Dennis "Den" Midgett of Manteo. Midgett, gentle and mentally challenged, was a square-jawed man of twenty-seven who wore his brown hair in a short brush cut. He had a heavy speech impediment. Teachers at the Manteo elementary school lacked the training to give him the special education he needed. Midgett dropped out of school. He did odd jobs at the Casino nightclub in Nags Head, and he was Manteo's unofficial town watchman, known for checking the doors of stores downtown late at night to make sure they were locked. He often talked to county deputies and Manteo police. He also drank beer and hung out with the late-night crowd, including Whaley. Midgett was given to asking friends, "How you doing, old buddy, old pal?" Everybody loved him.

At first glance, Midgett and Whaley didn't seem a natural fit. Midgett was working class and stuck to the basics in his conversations. Whaley was upper middle class and freely chatted up his prep school and college connections. But they both were looking for belonging on the island, boys who numbed their alienation with beer and couldn't stand to be alone in the hours before dawn as their friends turned in.

On the night Brenda vanished, Midgett told law enforcement officers, he'd been riding around with Whaley in Brenda's neighborhood. Whaley had told him he "had to have him a woman before he went to bed," Midgett said.

Dennis Midgett, Manteo's beloved "town watchman," provided information on the case. Photo from later in his life. *Courtesy the Midgett family.*

There was more. Whaley used to drive a 1964 two-door blue Valiant, but it had broken down on Hatteras Island on July 6. He had it towed back to Manteo and traded it for another car, and it was now at a garage. Robert Midgett, who reported the "ungodly scream" near his house at the time Brenda vanished, had said he heard a car with some type of engine trouble.

Agent Charlie Ray checked with the wrecker driver who towed in Whaley's car. The car's rear end had completely come apart, the driver said, and the drive shaft had dropped out on the ground. Ray asked the driver how the car would have sounded before it broke down. It would have been making a lot of noise, the driver said.

Agents Ray and Dan Gilbert went to the garage where Whaley's former car was stored and got permission from the garage operator to search it. On the seats and floorboard, they picked up and preserved in packages blond hair. The agents vacuumed the entire interior of the car and packaged and labeled those sweepings for future comparison to Brenda's hair.

The SBI agents went over their findings on Whaley with Sheriff Cahoon. Agent Lenny Wise said that Whaley, "at the moment, was a very good suspect."

Cahoon and the agents were also hearing about other suspects. Dr. Linus Matthew Edwards lived less than a quarter mile from Whaley in Mother Vineyard. Agent Jack Thomas would soon write this about Edwards in the SBI file on the case: "Investigation reveals [Edwards] as a possible suspect in as much as he was reportedly intoxicated and quite violent on the night of this crime. Further, that he left his home in search of his wife who fits the general description of Brenda Holland."

EDWARDS WAS A DENTIST. He stood six feet, two inches tall and weighed 195 pounds, mostly muscle but with a bit of a gut from drinking. His receding brown hair was going gray. He and Whaley knew each other only in passing. Like Whaley, Edwards could get out of control when drinking. Edwards was in his mid-forties, more than twice Whaley's age. Like Whaley, he had lived in Durham and had a high IQ. He boasted of belonging to Mensa, the group for those who score in the upper 2 percent of the general population in intelligence testing. And like Whaley, he was in Manteo looking for a new start, having never gotten over his own troubled childhood as the son of a Durham dentist and a demanding mother known as "Miss Bess." He burned over his strict parents shipping him off from their big house to a military school at an early age.

The son, who was born on March 7, 1916, graduated from dental school at Northwestern University in Chicago. In 1936, he married Ida Welch. He served in the U.S. Army during World War II in Germany, doing reconstructive surgery on soldiers with jaw injuries. He stayed in the army after the war. He arrived in Manteo around 1962 with his wife, fresh out

Dr. Linus Edwards, Manteo's only dentist and a suspect in the case, in front of his soundfront home in the late 1960s. *Courtesy Claudia Fry Sluder Harrington.*

of eighteen years in the army as a dentist, most recently stationed in South Carolina. He had attained the rank of lieutenant colonel. Along the way, he and Ida had divorced and then remarried. Edwards, through his dental connections in North Carolina, realized the unique opportunity that Manteo offered: It lacked a dentist. He and Ida, who had two grown children, settled into a house in Mother Vineyard. Ida Edwards was blond, tall, slender and kind; she favored capri pants and had polished nails.

Her husband opened a practice in a small building just off U.S. 64 and developed a thriving business. Within a year or so after their arrival, he and his wife divorced again.

By early 1964, Dr. Edwards was dating Dotty Fry. He was an outsider, and she was the ultimate insider, an alluring, kind and fun-loving woman who carried the oldest and proudest bloodlines of Roanoke Island.

DOTTY AND THE WAYWARD BUS

Dorris Elizabeth "Dotty" Fry was from a clan of industrious survivors that went back generations on Roanoke Island on her maternal side. Her mother, Cora Mae Basnight, was a local legend through her performances as the American Indian character "Agona" in *The Lost Colony*.

Dotty was born on May 13, 1932. Like Cora Mae's younger children, Dotty took her part in the *Lost Colony* crew, playing an American Indian. From the time Dotty was a child, her maternal grandmother, Belva Daniels, promoted her good looks. By the time Dotty was a teenager, she was a favorite of Aycock Brown. He shot numerous photos of her, some of which went nationwide, that highlighted her soft features, long legs and flowing locks, frequently dyed blond. She posed in swimsuits by the sea and up on the dunes, often with garlands of flowers around her neck. In one shot for an annual celebration, The Pirate's Jamboree, her hands are secured through a wooden pillory. Dotty, her bare legs protruding from slots in the bottom of the pillory, manages a noble half smile. She was five feet, eleven inches tall—a simmering slim siren. Letters poured in for her. One was just addressed to "Dotty—Roanoke Island." Somehow, it made it to her.

Dotty, as carefree as the windblown sea oats on the dunes she loved, was the visage landlocked men nationwide craved. She was known to everyone as just "Dotty." She was a fun-loving flirt who would fix a man with her eyes as blue as the ocean on a calm summer day and make him feel like she was the only one in the room worth talking to.

Legendary Outer Banks photographer Aycock Brown with one of his favorite models, Dotty Fry. *Aycock Brown photo, courtesy of Claudia Fry Sluder Harrington.*

She was not a good student and was one course short of graduating from Manteo High School when she took a break to work in her grandfather's downtown department store, M.L. Daniels'. The high school principal came by the store one day and told her that she should go back to school because there was a new teacher there she'd like: a handsome man named Wayland Hannon Fry. He was from a successful farming family in Carthage, North Carolina, a five-hour drive southwest of Manteo. He was a graduate of Wake Forest College and a decorated army veteran of World War II, having been wounded in combat in Europe, and he planned to go on to law school. Fry was soft-spoken, gentle and a winning basketball coach.

Dotty went back to school. She started dating Fry, a trend then not unusual. After graduation, Dotty attended East Carolina University in Greenville but came back to Manteo to be with Fry. One morning in 1952, a friend told Fry that he might want to take a look at the *Coastland Times*. Fry opened the paper, wondering what his friend thought he should see, and immediately came upon a large photo of Dotty. Right there in black and white were words that were news to him: an announcement that Wayland

Hannon Fry was engaged to Dorris Elizabeth Alford. He had not proposed to her. Dotty had taken out the announcement on her own. Dotty was Dotty. And Fry loved her for being her unpredictable self.

They were married on July 20, 1952, at Mount Olivet United Methodist, Dotty's family church in downtown Manteo. The groom was twenty-seven. The bride was twenty. Fry put his dream of law school aside and embraced teaching and building a family with his wife. Dotty, a whirlwind typist, worked as a secretary for Westvaco at their office in downtown Manteo. They rented a place in town as they had a cottage built in South Nags Head. When the construction was done, that cottage on the west side of the Beach Road near Whalebone Junction became their home. There they entertained friends, including Andy Griffith and his first wife, Barbara.

In March 1958, Dotty gave birth to a son. On June 4, 1959, after Dotty and Wayland had been married just seven years, Fry died of a heart attack while he and Dotty were visiting his family in Carthage. Shortly thereafter, Dotty's doctor confirmed that she was pregnant again. She didn't know whether she was emotionally prepared to handle another child.

But just like her mother, who'd been widowed with a new child on the way, Dotty was a survivor. She realized that she had to go through with the pregnancy. She named the baby Claudia after the doctor who delivered her, Claude Fletcher Bailey of Elizabeth City.

DOTTY CARRIED ON AS best she could, including by continuing the tradition started by her mother, that of the family staying active in *The Lost Colony*. Claudia played Virginia Dare, the first English child born in America, for two whole seasons, those of 1960 and 1961. She was the only baby to play little Virginia for that length of time. Aycock Brown snapped shots of Claudia swaddled in white linen as the baby Virginia.

By early 1964, Dotty was dating Linus Edwards. Her husband had been even-tempered, calm and gentle. Edwards was mercurial, hyper and rough.

Dotty and Linus Edwards married on August 22, 1964. He was forty-eight. She was thirty-two. Claudia, four years old, served as flower girl, sprinkling the church floor with petals. After the ceremony, Edwards made her go back and pick up each petal.

The new family settled into a soundfront house in Mother Vineyard that Edwards was buying from his next-door neighbors, Bill and Emma Lee

Crumpacker. The Edwards house was long and low with a white finish, designed for maximum views of the sound from almost every window. The dentist called it "Swan Haven." From inside the double wooden doors, across the foyer and living room, you could see the sound and all its color-shifting moods, and across the water was Jockey's Ridge. It was a quiet, secluded neighborhood. Claudia often played with the neighborhood children, including those of Andy Griffith, who lived in a soundfront home just up the sound from Mother Vineyard.

It seemed like a good life. But it was undergirded by strange scenes and brutality. While Edwards, whom Claudia called "Papa Doc," could be pleasant, he often simmered and boiled. He sometimes walked around nude, proud of his body. One night, Claudia was awakened by strange noises. She walked down the hallway and looked into the kitchen. Edwards had tied her mother to a table. The frightened child ran back to her bedroom and shut the door.

Edwards carried on an affair with a local woman, often meeting her at a beach motel on afternoons. Once, Dotty and her best friend, returning home unexpectedly from a shopping trip in Norfolk, Virginia, came upon Dr. Edwards and his mistress in the act on the family's living room couch.

Edwards demanded loyalty from Dotty and didn't want her to have any friends, male or female. He routinely insulted her best female friend.

Dotty Fry, even as Dotty Fry Edwards, would not be restrained by Dr. Linus Edwards. *Aycock Brown photo, courtesy Claudia Fry Sluder Harrington.*

Edwards often drank vodka and beer to excess and rained physical abuse on Dotty, at least once to the point that she had to be hospitalized. Other times she fled and hid in the homes of Emma Lee Crumpacker and other neighbors. She also took refuge at her mother's house. Dotty didn't report the incidents to law enforcement because she feared her husband. He was insanely jealous of her, including over her friendship with one of Danny Barber's housemates, Earl Mirus, with whom she worked at Westvaco.

But while she didn't report the abuse, Dotty stood up to Edwards. She had a deceptively fierce spirit. She kept seeing her friends, even if she might be beaten to hell for doing so. That summer of 1967, she had cut her hair into a bob and dyed it blond again. She was thirty-five but looked twenty-five. The town and the beach were hers. She wheeled around in a van with "The Wayward Bus" painted on the side (the title of a 1947 novel by John Steinbeck about strangers on a journey as well as a 1957 movie based on the novel) and sometimes in friends' convertibles.

Sheriff Cahoon knew Dotty and Dr. Edwards. By late July 1967, three weeks after Brenda's body was found, Cahoon was hearing more talk implicating Edwards. Some locals said the sheriff and Edwards were friends. Others just said that the sheriff was friendly to all his constituents. On July 21, Sheriff Cahoon relayed this information about Dr. Edwards to the SBI agents:

> *I received information that on Friday night, June 30, Dr. Edwards and his wife had some domestic difficulties. Dotty left home shortly after dark....Dr. Edwards started looking for Dotty Friday night or early Saturday morning. He's lived in Manteo for five years and has a very good business. He has a very poor reputation for excessive drinking. He operates a Ford Fairlane and is wearing a cast as a result of some difficulty he had recently. Dotty is the type of individual that would not be free to discuss her relationship with her husband to others and it's doubtful she would talk to investigating officers relative to her husband's behavior.*

The investigators concentrated on other suspects.

THE THING IN THE CASKET

Lola Mae Barnette told investigators that bloody clothes possibly related to Brenda's case, taken from John Davis Scarborough's station wagon, might be found in the home of John Langston Daniels. In his bedroom, she said, there was "a hole cut in the floor and a coffin-type thing under the house."

—note from August 1967 in the SBI file on Brenda's case

As the investigation dragged on that summer, it was obvious that it was 1967 in the South. While North Carolina, under Governor Terry Sanford in the early 1960s, had led the rest of the South in generally peaceful integration, that was a low bar. North Carolina had its share of stumbles in race relations, one of them massive. In the early 1960s, as most states backed off their programs of forced sterilization, North Carolina ramped up its eugenics program, concentrating on Black women and girls of modest means to reduce the welfare rolls. Some of the victims were bullied into operations that would leave them with physical and mental scars. North Carolina's program wouldn't end until 1974.

Against that backdrop, a citizen in the summer of 1967 wrote to Governor Dan Moore, a supposedly moderate Democrat, and the racist letter with a crackpot theory on Brenda's case received prompt and warm replies from the governor and SBI director Myron McBryde.

The July 12 letter writer was from Warrenton, in Western North Carolina, the mountainous region from which Brenda and the governor had come. In a weirdly Victorian tone, the man wrote of Brenda:

During her lonely walk in the direction of her home, if that was her intention and objective, could it not have been possible and probable that some lowly and partly intoxicated ruffians, possibly colored, having only a short while earlier had left some "depraved" night spot in the swamps, come upon this unprotected girl in the shadows and during her obviously brave walk to protect her honor from possibly unfair judgment concerning her situation, from an appearance standpoint, that she had only momentarily departed from?

…I trust that this letter is not deemed inappropriate, but reading that the young victim of the distressing tragedy was from this fine and fair area of our state, not too far from your former home, perhaps caused me to attempt to help, in this humble way of communicating to you, and hoping that intensified and more expert investigative efforts regarding the above case would continue.

With its careful drop-in of "possibly colored," the letter was a subtle dog whistle. The writer was making Brenda out to be a symbol of white purity threatened by Black ruffians, just as, starting in the late 1800s, white supremacists had begun to make the lost colony's Virginia Dare, the first English child born in America, a white angel threatened by American Indians.

Governor Moore, in a letter dated two days later, thanked the writer for his "thoughtful comments and suggestions" and wrote that he was forwarding Burton's letter to McBryde "for his attention and consideration." McBryde, in a letter dated July 21, told the writer that he appreciated his concern and assured him that "our Bureau is doing everything within our power to assist the Sheriff of Dare County in solving this tragic case." McBryde had taken a special interest in the case and was copied on many of the field agents' reports. As he replied to the letter writer, he copied one of those agents' supervisors, C.M. Bryan.

Soon after the governor and McBryde sent their letters, reports from the agents in the field reflected that they had begun investigating two Black suspects, based on allegations made by the alcoholic white lover of one of those men. Whether the timing was coincidental or not, the racial aspect of the probe was on.

Lola Mae Barnette was thirty-five and burned out. She lived in Frisco, a tiny town on the southern end of Hatteras Island. The slender island between the Pamlico Sound and the Atlantic composes Dare County's southern Outer Banks, separated from the northern banks by Oregon Inlet. On the morning of Tuesday, August 1, 1967, in his office, Sheriff Cahoon told SBI agents Lenny Wise and Dan Gilbert, according to their notes, that Barnette, "a white female of Frisco, has been reported to me as living with a Negro man by the name of John Langston Daniels in the [Manteo] area where the pocketbook was found belonging to Brenda Holland, and that I believe that Lola Mae Barnette might have information reference to a John Davis Scarborough being in the area on the morning of July 1, 1967 at about 2 to 3 a.m." That was the time frame in which Brenda vanished.

Late that Tuesday afternoon, Cahoon and Agent Wise left Manteo and rode down the banks to Frisco to talk to Barnette, crossing the high and winding Bonner Bridge over Oregon Inlet. The bridge had opened just four years before, replacing a ferry. The lawmen exited the bridge and proceeded onto Hatteras Island on N.C. Highway 12, a two-lane ride through low dunes, with the ocean and sound sometimes visible from either side.

The trip from Manteo took about forty-five minutes, with Cahoon driving and Wise riding shotgun. Talk came easily between the two friends, who shared the brogue and years of working together. Their native county was changing. Compared to the northern Banks, Hatteras Island was still the frontier. But there was good summer traffic, meaning decent business for the restaurants, hotels and marinas scattered along N.C. 12. Tourists were coming in for the fishing and to see Cape Hatteras Lighthouse and the rest of the National Park Service land.

By 6:00 p.m., Cahoon and Wise were in Barnette's small house in Frisco. With sunset still more than two hours away, soft beams streamed through the windows. Barnette sat down with the lawmen in her kitchen. She was chain-smoking, nervous because she was jonesing for a drink and because she knew that the white officers couldn't have approved of her relationship with a Black man. Just two months ago, the U.S. Supreme Court, in *Loving v. Virginia*, had struck down all state laws banning interracial marriage, but interracial relationships were still very much frowned on in the South.

Cahoon and Wise made clear to Barnette that her love affair wasn't their business, but what her Black boyfriend might have done to Brenda Holland was. Barnette began to talk. That day, and in another statement a few days later, she informed on her lover, John Langston Daniels, a laborer who was forty-four. He lived in a neighborhood bordering that of Danny Barber's.

Daniels's neighborhood was a Black section of Manteo that had been called "California" since it began as a community for freed slaves during the Civil War. The name derivation was uncertain, although some speculated that it meant that the land was a place of golden dreams for the freed slaves.

Barnette gave the investigators the following statement:

> *I was in the Manteo area on the night of June 30 and the early morning hours of July 1. I had been in the area for quite some time, living with John Langston Daniels. I'm an alcoholic and when I started drinking, I would go with anyone that would give me a drink. I had been living with John Langston Daniels at his home in the area where the pocketbook of Brenda Holland was found. On the night of June 30, I had been drinking wine and John Langston Daniels had been drinking some type of bourbon. I don't remember what time we went to bed, but I do remember at 2:30 to 3 a.m. in the early morning hours of July 1 that a blue-and-white station wagon pulled next to our bedroom window and the horn blew and John Langston Daniels got out of bed and went outside to the station wagon. I got up and looked out the window and saw John Davis Scarborough and another Negro male sitting in the front seat of the car and John Daniels opened the back door of the car and laid down in the back seat with what I believed to be a woman. I couldn't tell whether she was black or white. I heard John Davis Scarborough say to John Langston Daniels, "Do you think you can go back inside and sleep tonight?" I did not hear any other comments from him other than I heard him [Scarborough] say that was why he stuck with the same color. When John Langston Daniels came back into the house and to the bedroom and undressed to get back into bed, I saw three splotches of blood on his underpants. They were not there when he went outside to the car.*

When he returned from Hatteras, Agent Wise interviewed Scarborough at Cahoon's office in Manteo. Wise was joined by Agent Dan Gilbert. Scarborough began by saying, "I have not been to the home of John Langston Daniels in a long time. I don't hang around with people like that. I haven't drunk any liquor in the past eight or nine months. I don't know Lola Mae Barnette."

The agents pounced. "We have information you're lying," they said. "You do know Lola Mae and you were at John Daniels's home."

Finally, Scarborough admitted that he did know Barnette, that he knew she was a white woman living with John Daniels. But Scarborough insisted that he didn't go to Daniels's home in the early morning hours of July 1.

The agents kept pressing Scarborough about his "his alleged [*sic*] not remembering details of the night of June 30 and the early morning of July 1." Scarborough finally admitted that he had been out that night with a relative from out of town and that they'd gone to a Black bar in Manteo, Nick's House of Joy, and another beer joint. "I hadn't drank anything in nine or ten months and the whiskey hit me hard," he said. "I don't remember where we went after we left the last beer joint."

The agents wrote that Scarborough "violently denied being at John Daniels' home at 3:30 or anytime on the morning of July 1. He violently denied having any woman in the back of his station wagon although he stated he could not remember what happened that night."

With Scarborough still in the interview room, the agents had a deputy pick up John Langston Daniels and bring him to the sheriff's office. The agents brought Daniels into the room to confront Scarborough. Playing one suspect against the other was an old-school game, especially for white lawmen working Black suspects. Daniels told Scarborough, "You were at my house at 3:30 a.m. on July 1." Agent Gilbert then led Daniels out to question him in another room. Daniels told Gilbert that Scarborough had pulled up to his house during the hours in question, but the only people in the car were Scarborough and his relative.

In the other interview room, Wise kept pressing Scarborough. Not too long ago in North Carolina, some white investigators routinely beat confessions out of Black suspects. That wasn't always true now. The suspect pushed back against the lawmen.

"I wasn't at John Daniels' house and I insist on a lie detector test," Scarborough told Wise. "Impound my car. Do whatever test you have to prove I did not have this woman in my car on July 1."

Wise told Scarborough not to take a lie detector test if he had anything to hide. He read Scarborough his Miranda rights. Scarborough "continued steadily during the interview to contend that he could not remember anything from 4 p.m. on June 30, 1967 to approximately 7 to 7:30 a.m. on July 1, 1967....Questioning of this suspect continued until it was apparent that he would not change his story about the early morning hours of July 1, 1967," Wise wrote in the file on Brenda's case.

The agents let Scarborough and Daniels go home. Scarborough walked proudly out. The investigators impounded his 1960 Chevrolet station wagon for testing by an SBI chemist. They made plans to check out his story with his relative and to make another run at Lola Mae Barnette.

The SBI agents interviewed Lola Mae Barnette's relatives and friends about what she'd told them about the night in question. They found numerous holes in Barnette's story. She'd told one friend that she thought the woman in the back of Scarborough's station wagon was not white, but rather a Black woman she knew. That woman denied being in the car.

Barnette's brother, Hubert Ambrose, told Agent Charlie Ray that his sister "has had a drinking problem for some time. She has had hallucinations before when starts drinking excessively."

But Lola Mae Barnette wasn't done. She told investigators that bloody clothes taken from Scarborough's station wagon and possibly related to Brenda's case might be found in the home of John Langston Daniels. In his bedroom, she said, there was "a hole cut in the floor and a coffin-type thing under the house." Cahoon and Agents Lenny Wise and Dan Gilbert went to Daniels's house and asked his permission to search. "Go ahead," Daniels said, no warrant needed. Wise's report on what they found is surprisingly wry:

> *This hole in the floor was opened and there writer* [Lenny Wise] *and Agent Gilbert discovered Lola Mae Barnette in this box completely nude and in a very drunken condition. Sheriff Frank Cahoon was called to the room and there shown Lola Mae Barnette and he did not do anything reference removing her from the house. It is believed that Lola Mae Barnette was so drunk that she did not realize she was discovered in this condition.*

"I Did Not Kill
the Holland Girl"

Mr. Holland stated that he was coming to Manteo to kill the person responsible for his daughter's death. That the investigating officers were doing little to solve the crime.

—an August 5, 1967 passage in the SBI file on Brenda's case

August 5, 1967, was a Saturday. Shotgun Holland was sitting in his father's rocking chair in his basement in Canton, the bunker he'd been retreating to more and more. It was 5:45 p.m., safely into cocktail time, but Holland and the pain that ate at him, that thing inside him, didn't care about such social mores if he was off from his job as a floor supervisor at the local paper mill. He hunkered down in his bunker, drinking Pabst Blue Ribbon beer and Schlitz (like the ad said, "When you're out of Schlitz, you're out of beer") until he shifted to bourbon. He tried to watch the TV news. But up in his mountains, there were few news reports about his sweet Brenda anymore. Instead, the hippie war protesters filled his screen. Shotgun changed the channel. He watched westerns. He wanted to deliver justice like John Wayne in the movies, Sheriff Matt Dillon on the *Gunsmoke* TV show, the Barkley family in *The Big Valley* or the Cartwrights in *Bonanza*. There was this one episode of *Bonanza* from a few years earlier in which a little girl with blond pigtails escaped as killers murdered her parents. Hoss Cartwright took the girl in as the killers stalked her, believing that she carried a doll with money sewn inside it. Minutes before the show ended, one of the killers was threatening the girl when Hoss Cartwright charged in on his horse, jumped off and took out the killer. The girl looked like Brenda when she was little.

The shows Shotgun Holland absorbed were set in times out west less than a century before. He'd never gotten out to those high rocky canyons and deserts of cactus. But he knew what justice should look like. He'd seen it firsthand gunning down Nazis "Over There." He put himself in his western heroes' image, charging in like Hoss Cartwright at the last minute, pulling his revolver and filling his daughter's attacker with holes just as that man started to strangle Brenda. Shotgun would have, could have saved her, by God. He didn't even want to think about what the attacker had done to his daughter before that point. Shotgun Holland was just over twenty years past his world war, where good supposedly won over evil. But that ideal was shifting as fast as those sands down there where Brenda was killed. The newspapers said that Danny Barber was a U.S. Army vet, but Shotgun Holland knew that boy hadn't seen combat like he had. Singing in the army band in safe spots like Barber had didn't get it.

All Shotgun Holland had left was wanting to be the dark angel avenger for his daughter. In his mountains, killers were ferreted out, one way or the other, and dealt with. Why the hell wasn't that happening in Manteo?

Sometimes the buzz hit his fingertips and he'd call someone on his rotary-dial phone. That Saturday afternoon at about 5:45 p.m., he dialed the Dare County Sheriff's Office in Manteo. SBI agent Lenny Wise noted the call in Brenda's file:

> *On August 5, 1967, at 6 p.m., Agent O.L. Wise received a telephone call from radio dispatcher Elma Wood advising that she received a telephone call from victim's father, Mr. Holland, at approximately 5:45 p.m. August 5, 1967 and that Mr. Holland sounded as if he had been drinking and was under the influence of alcohol. Mr. Holland stated that he was coming to Manteo to kill the person responsible for his daughter's death. That the investigating officers were doing little to solve this crime. That Mr. Holland appeared to be very upset, that he did not state when he was coming to Manteo, nor who he intended to kill.*

Lenny Wise probably entered the passage in the file to cover himself just in case Shotgun did roll in. Wise, a father from modest rural roots himself, probably understood Holland's feelings. But Wise knew that the world was changing. Just last year, the Miranda decision had come down. Sheriff Cahoon grumbled about such legal niceties. "I do believe that if we could pick up some of the suspects and let them sweat it out in jail for a couple of days, the guilty person would talk plenty," he told the United Press International news service in the late summer of 1967. "But we can't do that, so we'll just have to work it out some other way."

In an interview with the *Charlotte Observer*, the sheriff indicated that the investigation wasn't all it should be. "Right from the beginning, hundreds of well-wishers wanted to help search for the body," he said. "They wanted to search the woods. I couldn't turn them down, but I had to organize them, and that took time when I should have been doing other things."

By August 1967, the sheriff, privately, had one main suspect—Danny Barber—and he wanted him to feel like the heat was solely on him. Cahoon told Shotgun Holland in phone calls that Barber was the key suspect, and Holland was forever out for Barber. When Holland told that dispatcher he was coming to Manteo to kill the person responsible for Brenda's death, it was clear he meant Barber.

THAT AUGUST, THE SBI investigators explored the movements of Barber and several other suspects in the predawn hours when Brenda vanished. They included the Black suspects; Dr. Edwards; and David Whaley, the other suspect from Mother Vineyard. Cahoon had written a letter to FBI director J. Edgar Hoover introducing several items of Brenda's to be compared with sweepings from Whaley's car. FBI forensic scientists found that blond hair from Whaley's car "compared favorably" with hairs from Brenda. And Manteo's unofficial night watchman, Dennis Midgett, had told investigators that Whaley had been riding around Barber's neighborhood when Brenda vanished.

On Tuesday, August 1, Lenny Wise and Supervising Agent Fentress drove Whaley to the Ocean House. The setting of the interview at the motel, a twenty-minute drive from Manteo, was an attempt to battle the rumors swirling around the case. Cahoon and the agents continued to interview suspects in Cahoon's Manteo office. But when they had time, the lawmen did their interviews at the Ocean House. That location might also have been a way to sell the suspects on talking—there was less chance of Manteo locals seeing them going into an interview there.

Fentress read the suspect his Miranda rights. Whaley was nineteen, a hard-drinking boy in that time when one could legally buy beer at eighteen.

His grandfather was the rector of St. Andrew's Episcopal Church in Nags Head. Whaley told the agents that he'd heard from his grandfather that he was a suspect in the case. His grandfather most likely heard that from his friend Aycock Brown, who was a lay leader at St. Andrew's. Whaley continued:

> *I talked to my grandfather over a week ago, and he told me there were rumors of me having a late date with Brenda Holland on July 1. I was shocked to hear that. That's untrue. I didn't know Brenda Holland. On Friday night, July 30, I believe I was at the Casino until after midnight. I know I had about four or five beers that night and came back to Manteo and rode around town. This was about 2 a.m. I picked up Dennis Midgett. We rode downtown together to the Midway service station and bought some gas, and Dennis paid for it. We left there and rode through the backroads of Manteo, including the area around Danny Barber's house. We also rode through the colored section. I wasn't especially looking for "a pick-up" or a woman, but I just liked to ride around at night when I didn't feel like going home. We drank beer while we were riding around. I went by where Danny Barber lives two or three times at around 3:30 to 3:45 a.m. but I didn't see any car that I remember or any person walking on the road. I dropped Dennis Midgett off about 4 a.m. and, to the best of my knowledge, went straight home. On July 4, I went to Hatteras and on the way back the rear end in my car came out, the drive shaft came out and fell on the ground. I left the car there and had a wrecker pull the car in. The following Saturday, I got a newer car, a 1965 Oldsmobile.*

The agents asked Whaley about Rodney Brett. Brett worked at the Carolinian Hotel in Nags Head. Whaley had worked there the summer before. Whaley said he knew Brett but had seen him only one time since Brenda was slain and that Brett had "very little" to say. He's "not all there," Whaley told the agents. They pressed him for more details about his movements on the night Brenda disappeared. He told them:

> *On July 1, during the early morning hours while I was riding around with Dennis Midgett, I had 12 to 15 beers. I was not drunk but I was feeling good. I often drink a lot of beer and do so almost every day. My mother knows I drink beer and that I'm old enough to. I drink it around the house. I wouldn't have been afraid to go home because I'd been drinking.*

The agents moved on Whaley. A blond hair was found in your old car that could be Brenda's hair, they told him. Whaley couldn't explain what the hair was doing in his car but said, "I don't know anything about this case. I'm innocent and I'll take a lie detector test anytime to clear this up." The agents told him not to take the test if he had anything to hide.

In response to more questioning, Whaley added that before picking up Dennis Midgett, he'd gone to a party at a Manteo apartment where four girls lived. There, he said:

> *A boy borrowed my car to take his girl home. He brought my car back about 1:30 a.m. That's when I went downtown and picked up Dennis. I don't remember telling Dennis that I had to have a woman before I went to bed, but I could have. One of the reasons I was riding around Colored Town was that I went by two colored beer joints to try to buy beer but couldn't.*

The agents asked Whaley about the girls he had dated that summer. He named four, including one who had light blond hair. He'd made out with her in his old car, Whaley said.

The investigators wound the questioning to a close. "Don't leave town without calling us," they told him. Whaley told them he'd be ready for more questioning or a lie detector test anytime.

The agents followed up with the man Whaley had loaned his car to. That man said his date who got in the car with him was a blonde.

Something about Whaley still gave the agents an uneasy feeling. He had, by his own admission, been in Danny Barber's neighborhood at the time Brenda disappeared, drinking like crazy and wanting to find a woman. They'd keep looking at him.

ABOUT THE SAME TIME the agents were interviewing Whaley that Tuesday, Sheriff Cahoon got a call at his office from his optometrist, Ray Stoutenburg. The doctor told the sheriff that he needed his glasses changed and to come over. When Cahoon got to the downtown Manteo office, he found out the doctor had an ulterior motive. He had information to share about Dr. Linus Edwards's actions around the time Brenda went missing. The doctor lived a few houses up from Edwards. He told Cahoon:

On Saturday, July 1, at about 2:15 a.m. I was awakened by a loud noise in and around Dr. Edwards' home. I heard Dr. Edwards' voice and a woman that I assumed by to be Mrs. Edwards. Dr. Edwards was cursing and using abusive language and a short time later I heard a car leave. I thought that to be Mrs. Edwards. After she had been gone about 15 minutes, Dr. Edwards' car left. All the lights were left on inside and outside the house. It was a real dark night and I could not see much but I could hear practically all that was said.

The eye doctor said that when he went to work a few minutes after 8:00 a.m. that Saturday, he saw the car of Dr. Edwards's mistress parked behind the doctor's car. The cars were still there when he came home for lunch, he said, and when he closed his office that Saturday afternoon, the car of the mistress was gone. But the next morning, when he started for Sunday school, he said, the car of the mistress was back at Dr. Edwards's house. About midafternoon, he said, the mistress came over to his house, and he and his wife "could tell by her appearance that she was very much disturbed about something." The mistress, he said, said that "Dr. Edwards was very nervous and upset and he was going to close his office and leave Manteo." Stoutenburg said he told her, "Why, he can't do that, he's like I am, he's invested too much money in his office and, also, what would Manteo do?" The mistress spoke up and said there was a lot more involved than just that and stated, "I believe I have talked too much."

The eye doctor ended with this: "Dr. Edwards is a very nervous person and very vicious when he's drinking. I've played cards with him and he would always show his temper if he were losing. I will talk to the agents investigating the Brenda Holland case, but contact would have to be made by phone so agents would not be seen around my office or my home."

The optometrist was not alone in his fear of Edwards. One of the dentist's sons-in-law, William J. "Bill" Watson Jr., was also talking to agents in secret. Watson told agents that Edwards was very violent and dangerous when drinking. But most importantly, Watson said that Edwards was jealous of his wife's friendship with Earl Mirus, who worked with her at Westvaco and lived with Barber.

Dotty Edwards sometimes stopped by the house to visit Mirus. The dentist may have driven around Barber's neighborhood looking for his wife around the time Brenda disappeared, when Robert Midgett heard the scream.

IN MID-AUGUST, THE SBI brought in Agent John Vanderford to conduct a series of polygraph tests in room 38 of the Ocean House. The key questions would be about Brenda's disappearance and slaying. The agents started with Barber at 3:00 a.m. on Monday, August 14. The early morning timing must surely have been meant to catch him off guard. "Deception was detected on the test on relevant questions," the agents noted in the file. They did not go into details.

The next day, Vanderford gave polygraph tests to Barber's housemates, Rodney Brett and Earl Mirus. By then, agents had investigated Mirus's story about going to see his girlfriend in New Jersey around the time Brenda disappeared. His story checked out. The agents noted that "no deception was detected" in the tests of Brett and Mirus. David Whaley also took the test that day. Once more, the agents noted that "no deception was detected."

Finally, on August 16, Vanderford gave one of the Black suspects, John Davis Scarborough, a polygraph test. Scarborough had vehemently denied the claims made by the white woman, alcoholic Lola Mae Barnette, that he had somehow been involved in Brenda's slaying. In his testing, just as those of all the suspects so far except Barber, "No deception was detected." SBI forensic agents had tested his car and found nothing to link it to Brenda.

DR. EDWARDS WAS DRUNK, and he had something to say at the sheriff's office. It was dusk on Friday, August 18. The big dentist, his pants pulled up past his waist and his thick-lensed glasses not hiding his vodka-washed eyes, stormed into the first floor of the courthouse and started rambling on to the dispatcher about the Brenda Holland case, running his hands through his spare hair. Dispatcher Elma Wood, double-clutching between sending a handful of deputies to the drunk calls pouring in from fish shacks on the mainland and bars on the beach, stopped what she was doing and called Sheriff Cahoon at home, telling him that Edwards was there and that he had better come talk to him. Cahoon got there moments later. As he entered the main lobby, he could hear Edwards talking loudly to the dispatcher: "I did not kill the Brenda Holland girl and I don't know who did. Investigators got the dates confused. I was not out that Friday night but was out and at the sheriff's office that Saturday night, July 1, talking to Deputy Sheriff Will Daniels. Daniels made a phone call to my wife's people for me."

Edwards rambled on until he saw Cahoon. He turned from the dispatcher to the sheriff and said, "I did not kill the Holland girl. The rumor got started at the sheriff's office, and it's about to ruin my business and marriage."

Cahoon told the dentist the rumor didn't start at his office, but he had heard it. "I think you should go on home and go on back to work, as you have been doing, and try to forget the rumor," the sheriff said.

Edwards stalked out of the courthouse. Cahoon waited a few minutes and followed him out. Then the sheriff and the local Ford dealer, R.D. Sawyer, drove Edwards home. On the way there, the sheriff told the SBI agents, Edwards "was quite congenial and had nothing further to say about the Brenda Holland case."

The sheriff failed to say why he didn't get Edwards into an interview room to talk more about his alibi.

SÉANCES AND THE SUPERNATURAL

At the séance… [Houston Rob Waters] *immediately said "water" or "rope" or "ask a question about rope" and stated, "that was what Brenda Holland was killed by."*

—*from an August 27, 1967 passage in the SBI file on Brenda's case*

In a July 8, 1967 letter to Brenda's parents, a North Carolina woman suggested they turn to Jeane Dixon, a popular psychic and astrologist. Dixon, born Lydia Emme Pinkert in Wisconsin, was one of ten children of Catholic parents who'd come to America from Germany. Dixon was raised in Michigan and California and once said that a "gypsy" she'd met in childhood had forecast her gift. She gained fame after President Kennedy's assassination in 1963, when it was noted that she'd written in *Parade* magazine in 1956 that the Democratic winner of the 1960 presidential race would be assassinated. She later predicted that Republican Richard Nixon would win the 1960 election. But in an era where many Americans craved counsel from the stars and beyond, Dixon's fans focused on what she got right rather than what she got wrong.

By the summer of 1967, she was a household name with a syndicated column and best-selling book whose fans included Nixon and his wife, Pat. Dixon, who remained a Catholic, was on the conservative, mainstream side of the supernatural world, dressing modestly, with her dark hair carefully coifed and a necklace bearing a small cross around her neck.

Brenda's parents never took up the letter writer's suggestion to seek out Jeane Dixon. But her brand of predictions was widely accepted, part of a wider trend. "Extrasensory perception" (ESP), involving the reception of predictions and information beyond the physical senses, as well as "reincarnation," the belief that spirits are reborn as new people with memories of past lives, became catchwords. Studies at Duke University in North Carolina were validating ESP. Manteo's Andy Griffith was winking at the trend. In 1965, a segment of his namesake show had bumbling Deputy Warren Ferguson (Barney Fife's replacement) using his supposed ESP to predict that Andy's picnic with his girlfriend, Helen, would end in a bad accident. By 1972, even the TV western *Bonanza* would feature an episode in which a psychic helped find a wounded man.

But the supernatural world of the late 1960s still included many souls out of the mainstream, like Coy Dupree, a high school student whom SBI agent Jack Thomas interviewed. That was in Selma, a tobacco town in Johnston County, a three-hour drive southwest of Manteo. A few decades before, Ava Gardner had jumped out of the Johnston County community of Grabtown and put Frank Sinatra and much of the rest of the world under her sexy, hard-living spell.

The principal at the Selma High School had contacted the SBI as the 1967 school year started, saying that agents might want to interview Dupree, an eighteen-year-old who had worked at Nags Head that summer. "He's an odd person who seems to have death on his mind a good deal of the time," the principal told the SBI. Agent Thomas drove up to the school and had Dupree take a seat in his car. Dupree told Thomas that he'd told two beach friends he had killed Brenda but that he was "just kidding around." He said that he and other friends had tried, during a séance, to ask the spirit world about Brenda through a Ouija board. Those popular boards were marked with numbers and letters. Participants placed their hands on a small piece of wood or plastic called a "planchette" and supposedly let it move them, in response to questions about the dead, to spell out words and numbers. Dupree said he'd worked at the Cabana East hotel in Nags Head. Agent Thomas knew the place as a decent three-story oceanfront hotel of brick at the 11 Milepost on the Beach Road. "Tell me more," he said. Dupree made the following statement:

> *I'm a junior here at Selma High. My hobbies are oil painting and poetry. I'm on probation for breaking and entering, and was suspended from school once for getting smart with a teacher. I worked at the Cabana East from July*

11, 1967 until Sept. 5, 1967 as a desk clerk. I had a room at the motel with several other boys, also employees.…I didn't know Brenda Holland and never tried to meet her, but I did believe in ESP and reincarnation. One of the girls at the Cabana East was a medium for communicating with the dead. I was taking part in a séance at the hotel once and someone asked Ouija, "Who killed Brenda?" Ouija replied, "God has a message." About that time, a guy came in and the contact was broken…

Death interests me a great deal. I have thought about killing someone to see what reaction it would have on me. I have wondered how it would feel to kill my father or sister and whether or not I would cry. In asking myself this question, the answer is always no. I would like to see someone die just to see if I would be sorry and cry.…I didn't tell [my two beach friends] *how I might have killed Brenda because the conversation didn't go that far. I've never said I killed anyone else. Right after Brenda was killed, I and the other boys in my room kidded around about each of us having done it. I asked of them "Why did you kill that girl last night?"…I would really like to take a polygraph test, I think that would be interesting.*

The witching hour is 11:30 p.m. to midnight. Once, I had a love feast with champagne, two glasses, a candle and a mirror tying to communicate with a spirit, but I had negative results.

Thomas let the boy out of his car and drove away from the school. Dupree was off the wall indeed, but he was just one of many strange types the agents on Brenda's case had encountered. Another was Houston Rob Waters.

IT WAS LATE SATURDAY night on August 26, 1967, one of the last big party nights of the summer. The *Lost Colony* season was wrapping up that weekend. Many members of the company would be leaving the island. This was one of their last times to come together and gossip about Barber and Brenda and everything else that had happened in the last three months.

But Molly Black, a tippler who'd been Brenda's roommate, was sober that night. At 11:00 p.m., she placed an urgent call to the Dare County Sheriff's Office, telling the dispatcher that she had information she thought might be of interest regarding the Brenda Holland case. She asked that an agent contact her two and a half hours later, at 1:30 a.m., at her Manteo house. The dispatcher immediately called Sheriff Cahoon. Cahoon, in turn, called

SBI agent Lenny Wise at his room at the Ocean House. Shortly after 1:00 a.m., Wise picked up Cahoon at his office in downtown Manteo for the ride over to the house Molly Black shared with two other girls.

Black was a key witness who knew things about Brenda's last days, maybe more than she'd told them so far. Black was nervous, dramatic and fearful. She was also part of the *Lost Colony* clique that contended that their fellow crew member Danny Barber had nothing to do with the slaying.

As Cahoon and Wise sat down with Molly Black in her small living room, they quickly realized that she hadn't changed her mind about Barber. Her target was her ex-boyfriend, Houston Rob Waters, who had worked at Jennette's Pier. Black told the lawmen that earlier that night at work at *The Lost Colony*, she overheard a conversation about a séance at the Manteo home of a cast member. Waters was at the séance, she said, and he made some comments about Brenda's killing. The brother of one of her roommates, who was visiting from out of town, had been at the séance the previous Friday night, Black said, and he would talk to the lawmen.

"Sure," the sheriff and Wise said, "we'd like to hear from him." Black went in another room, led out a man in his twenties and introduced him to Cahoon and Wise. The man, Jay Fieldman, a graduate student at the University of Oregon, took a seat and re-created the séance that took place in a dark room. The host told everyone to sit down in a circle and hold hands. Fieldman continued:

> The host then lit a candle and placed it in the center of the circle and immediately started telling ghostly stories, and, in about thirty to forty-five minutes, a man started going under the spell and he broke out in a sweat and started moaning and groaning and then a woman seated a short distance from me stated or said the word "rope" and [Houston Waters] immediately said "water" or "rope" or "ask a question about rope" and stated that was what Brenda Holland was killed by, and then real quick said "or that was what the police had said."
>
> The séance was then broken up, but a short time later a second séance started. No one went under the spell during the second séance as far as I knew, but I didn't stay too long. I did hear [Houston Waters] during the second séance start crying and say that it was very sad about Brenda Holland.
>
> I didn't realize what was being said because I didn't know about Brenda Holland or about her death until last night. I don't believe in this thing they call a "séance." I only attended to see what it was all about and, in my opinion, no one was under any spell during the entire séance and, after

talking to people about the Brenda Holland case, nothing was said that had not been talked about or read in the newspaper.

Cahoon and Agent Wise would have had to agree with Fieldman on his last point, that of nothing being said at the séance that hadn't been in the newspapers. They bid goodnight to him and Molly Black.

EARLIER IN AUGUST, AGENTS Charlie Ray and Jack Thomas had followed up on the Houston Bob Waters angle. The most important thing they found was that Waters's boss said he had seen Waters retire to his room at the pier early on the morning that Brenda went missing; Waters had not had access to a car at that time. He was a bizarre person, one of many the agents were confronting in this case. But they didn't have nearly enough to put a murder charge on him.

Waters may have told his friend Rob Breeze about Brenda's date with Barber on the last night of her life. Breeze was the man who had left Brenda devastated after her date with him. One theory held that Breeze may have continued his pursuit of Brenda on the night she vanished. Breeze gave investigators an alibi they privately said was airtight. They did not go into details, nor did they press Breeze on statements made by Brenda and others about what happened between them sexually that caused Brenda to stop seeing him a week before she was slain. The lawmen, products of their time, would have taken the fact that she had not reported a sexual assault to them as evidence that it had not happened. Brenda, too, was a product of her time. She was raised in a culture that, in large part, could not conceptualize a woman being raped on a date. If anything untoward did occur, that culture said, the woman had probably enticed the man into it.

"I Can't Do Anything but Kill You"

It was September, a usually good time on the Outer Banks. The tourists were gone, those space invaders and traffic-jammers on which the locals depended but cursed in whispers. Locals were counting their summer earnings, hoping that they had enough money to make it to the next summer season but glad to spend a few bucks drinking with friends they'd hardly seen since the summer started. On the best days, the salty smell of the sea was damp and fresh, and the sun was out. In September 1967, as always, the sea oats were golden, and the Atlantic was still warm, often sporting whitecaps in late afternoon as the wind shifted. There were still plenty of calm days left before the banshee nor'easters of fall, affording ample opportunities for locals to gather on dunes by the sea, drink cool beer and ponder the summer. Everybody was still talking about "The Girl in the Sound." Locals would ride up Burnside Road, where Brenda had taken her last walk, and shiver. They debated their theories on the case—who might have killed her and why and how he was getting away with it. It was always "he." Nobody, lawmen or civilians, ever suspected a woman of being the killer. And most locals agreed that the male killer had acted alone.

Sheriff Cahoon and the team of SBI agents in Dare County, after a summer of chasing leads all over the place, were coming up empty. Forensic comparisons of Brenda's clothes and hair with samples from suspects' cars, tests done by the SBI and the FBI, had produced nothing of evidentiary value. Ditto for two pieces of rope, one that Aycock Brown had found in his front yard in Manteo and another that one of Dr. Edwards's sons-in-law, William Jesse "Bill" Watson Jr., had found in Edwards's boat soon after Brenda's body surfaced. Photos of Brenda's corpse, a basic for making any murder case, were also hitting a snag. The state trooper on the scene had sent his negatives to the Capital Camera Shop in Raleigh. The shop notified the SBI in August that all those exposures came out blank. The lawmen still had Aycock Brown's shots of the corpse.

That September, Danny Barber had gone back to school at Carolina. Some islanders backed the *Lost Colony* cohort in contending that Barber was innocent, even though one thing about him still bothered them: the fact he had failed Brenda by going to sleep, not saving her from that deadly walk home. For the old-line southerners of Manteo, that was just unchivalrous. Other islanders believed he was the killer.

With Barber back at school, the SBI agents finally took a hard look at Dr. Linus Edwards. He was known as a troubled drunkard who was insanely jealous of his wife, Dotty, and had torn out after her in the early morning darkness Brenda had faded into. Dotty and Brenda, both blond and slender, both with long necks, bore a strong resemblance to each other, some islanders kept saying. They contended that Edwards, jealous of his wife's friendship with one of Barber's housemates, may well have been driving around Barber's house, spotted Brenda walking and mistook her for Dotty on that dark road.

Cahoon and the SBI agents, for reasons uncertain, were skeptical of that theory, but they pursued it. They discerned that on the night and early morning hours in question, Dotty Edwards's two children from her first marriage were with their late father's kinfolk, a five-hour drive away in the rolling fields of Carthage, North Carolina. With the children away, Edwards lashed out at Dotty even more.

The chief instigator against Edwards was Watson. He was a hardy native of Ballinger, Texas, and U.S. Army veteran. He met his wife in his home state, and she led him to Manteo. Watson and his family lived in Mother Vineyard, just a few blocks away from Edwards's home with Dotty. Watson was six-foot, three-inches tall, with dark curly hair, fun-loving but, by turns, serious behind his thick-framed, army-issued glasses. He worked construction jobs, as a commercial fisherman and, for a while, as a highway engineer technician for the state. He loved Budweiser Tall Boys and strumming his guitar at home, occasionally with Andy Griffith. He hated bullies and considered his father-in-law one of them. He believed that Edwards may well have killed Brenda and made it his business to tell that to the law. He often clashed with Edwards in the weeks after

Brenda's body was found. Bill Watson wasn't scared of anything, and he was protective of his family.

Watson met with SBI agents in secret. That September, he told Agents Charlie Ray and Lenny Wise that Edwards was a paranoid schizophrenic who said he once caught his mother in bed with a man who was not his father. Edwards often talked of hating his parents, Watson said. Recently, he said, Edwards had hurt his back somehow, had surgery and gotten a prescription for Demerol from his other son-in-law, Manteo pharmacist Woody Fearing. Watson also gave the SBI agents a note that another man had given him. Dotty had apparently left the note at Danny Barber's house around the time Brenda vanished. The note, written in cursive, mentioned both of Barber's housemates, Rodney Brett and Earl Mirus. Dotty was friends with both men and worked with Mirus at Westvaco:

> *Rodney,*
>
> *I won't be gone late, am at the hill house. Be back around 2:00 a.m. Relax and sleep tight, Earl. Thanks for the beer, Rodney*
>
> *Dotty*

The note was not dated. But the agents had learned that there was a party at the Hill House, where some members of the *Lost Colony* company lived, during the hours in which Brenda vanished. And Dotty's best friend would later say that after Dotty fled her husband that night, she picked her up and they rode around, making a quick stop at Barber's house. Dotty went in alone. Brett wasn't home yet. Nor was Barber, out with Brenda. Mirus was asleep. Dotty apparently borrowed a beer and left the note. Edwards may have been searching for her and swung back through the neighborhood later.

In addition to working at Westvaco, Dotty was a notary public. Investigators could have easily compared the handwriting on the note with Dotty's other penmanship. That, apparently, was not done.

Agents Jack Thomas and Dan Gilbert checked with pharmacist Woody Fearing about the Demerol. He said he had filled a prescription for 100mg of Demerol for Dr. Edwards on July 26. Dr. Harvey, the town's only general practice doctor, wrote the prescription. Fearing said he didn't know the reason for the prescription, but it was his understanding that Edwards had hurt his neck. He had been wearing some type of body cast. Whether Dr. Edwards had hurt his back or his neck, and how, would remain unclear. Apparently,

Cahoon and the SBI agents never pressed for an answer, leaving a burning question: could the dentist have sustained an injury tossing Brenda's body over the high point of the bridge to Manns Harbor?

JEAN STOUTENBURG, WHO LIVED three houses up from Dr. Edwards in Mother Vineyard, had something to say. She was a petite Florida native, a graduate of the University of Miami and the wife of the town's optometrist. She was a mother in her mid-thirties. She and her husband, Raymond, had talked about Brenda's case and what they saw and heard in the days after Brenda vanished. Ray Stoutenburg, starting with the clandestine meeting with Sheriff Cahoon and proceeding to one with the SBI, had already given two statements. On Thursday, September 7, in her home, Jean Stoutenburg gave her own statement to Supervising Agent Clyde Fentress and Agent Jack Thomas. She corroborated her husband's account, including his statement that Dr. Edwards's mistress had been at his house on the weekend that Brenda went missing. And she said that after Edwards and his wife fought the Friday night of that weekend, Dotty didn't return to the house until the following Wednesday. She remembered that because Dr. Edwards had lashed out at his wife that day. Jean Stoutenburg told the agents:

> *The day before Brenda's body was found, I had a car title I wanted to get notarized. Dotty Edwards is a notary public and I wanted her to notarize it. I called her and she went downtown to get her notary stamp. While she was gone, I called her at home to ask for something else, not realizing she was gone. Dr. Edwards answered the phone and said Dotty was not there and slammed the phone down. A short while later, Dotty drove up in the yard and I could hear Dr. Edwards really chewing Dotty out for fooling around with notary public work. This was the first day I had seen Dotty back at home since the fight on Friday night, June 30. Dotty came over to my house in her van and notarized the title for me. I asked her about Earl Mirus leaving town. Dotty said, "Oh no, he's a nice boy." I told Dotty that she and Brenda favored quite a bit in appearance and even had the same color of hair.*

Jean Stoutenburg continued her statement, laying out her theory of the case and more:

> *From what I have seen and heard and know about the situation, I think it's quite possible that Dr. Edwards and Dotty had a fight on Friday night, June 30. Dotty left the house, en route to see Earl Mirus. Dr. Edwards on this particular Friday night went down near Danny Barber's house to watch for them. Perhaps he saw Brenda walking along the road and thought it was his wife and killed her.*

Jean Stoutenburg added this:

> *On August 25, I had a dental appointment with Dr. Edwards. I was afraid of him since all of these things had come about. I decided to go ahead and keep the appointment. When I got in the chair, I told Dr. Edwards not to hurt me. He replied, "I can't do anything but kill you."*

The dentist, aware of the rumors, was probably joking in his own dark way. But that did not alleviate Stoutenburg's fear or her belief that Edwards

Dr Linus Edwards's dental office in Manteo. *Courtesy Claudia Fry Sluder Harrington.*

quite probably killed Brenda. "I prefer this interview remain confidential," she told the agents in closing, "but should it come down to a court trial, I would be perfectly willing to go into court and testify to anything I have stated here."

THE SBI AGENTS PROBED Edwards's background. Stories about his bizarre and sometimes violent behavior, past and present, were washing over the island. A few years ago, Edwards had severely beaten a man over one of Edwards's affairs. The loser in that fight had confronted the dentist because he was having an affair with the loser's sister, SBI agents learned. Neighbors told the agents about Edwards drunkenly prowling around their yards and down by the town cemetery.

On Monday, September 11, Agents Dan Gilbert and Jack Thomas made the two-hour drive to Greenville, North Carolina, for an interview with Edwards's ex-wife, Ida Welch Edwards. She was a dormitory house mother at East Carolina University and was working toward a degree there. She was friendly and talkative, free from the shadow of her ex. She told the agents that she was married to Edwards from 1936 to 1956. They divorced but remarried in 1960, she said, and then divorced again about four years ago because "he had fallen in love with other girls." She also told the agents:

> *Dr. Edwards attempted suicide in Columbia, South Carolina, while he was in the service. At the time, he only had about three years to go on his military retirement but left the service anyway. He always said he left of his own accord, but I often wondered about that since he only had three years to go on retirement. The time he attempted suicide, he was having severe emotional problems, along with his drinking, and slashed his wrists. I carried him to the hospital. These things only occurred when he was drinking heavily.…He's an extremely jealous person and very possessive of his wife. I would be very much afraid if I was his wife and was being unfaithful to him. He always said that he could not remember what he did when he was drinking heavily.*
>
> *Dr. Edwards had great hostility toward his father and felt rejected because his father put him in a military academy at an early age. His mother is a very nice person but does not understand him.*

In the days ahead, the agents tracked down Edwards's military records, including those of his suicide attempt, which took place around 8:00 p.m. on November 17, 1960, at Fort Jackson in Columbia. On November 23, 1960, an investigating officer read Lieutenant Colonel Edwards his military rights and questioned him about the incident. Edwards said that he had been under psychiatric care for the past several months. "On the evening of 17 November, 1960 in my quarters in Columbia, I did inflict a wound on my left wrist," Edwards wrote. "This was under emotional duress."

A few months later, on March 31, 1961, Dr. Edwards received an honorable discharge from the army. Ida Edwards was right in wondering why the dentist had left the service just three years shy of a full military pension. Soon after they remarried and moved to Manteo, they divorced again, setting up his marriage to Dotty.

ISLANDS ARE INHERENTLY INSULAR. So it was Roanoke Island, its county seat of Manteo and its prominent families. They'd bled and sweated for generations to make a living, then a good living, from fishing and commercial development—and hand-in-hand with that development went *The Lost Colony*. Members of Dotty's close-knit clan served on the Manteo Town Council and the Dare County Board of Commissioners. Relatives of the Daniels side of the family owned and operated the *News & Observer*, based in Raleigh, the most powerful newspaper in the state through its fierce backing of the Democratic Party. Other relatives served in the state legislature. They didn't share family issues with outsiders. The family didn't like bullies, especially ones from out of town, and some of Dotty's relatives recognized soon after her 1964 marriage to Linus Edwards that he was one of those. They talked about him and loathed him. Cora Mae Basnight, Dotty's mother, privately called him "the Black Dragon." But talking to SBI investigators was a different thing. This was family business, not that of the outside world. The SBI agents, except for Lenny Wise, who'd grown up on mainland Dare County, were regarded warily by Dotty's kin.

Against that backdrop, it's significant that SBI agents Jack Thomas and Dan Gilbert scored an interview with Dotty's eighty-two-year-old grandmother, Belva Midgett Daniels, in her three-story Victorian house in downtown Manteo. She was a beloved anchor of the town and the widow of Moncie L. Daniels Sr., who started his namesake department store

Belva Midgett Daniels, Dotty's grandmother, talked to investigators about Brenda's case. *Courtesy Claudia Fry Sluder Harrington.*

downtown, as well as an oil and gas business. Belva Daniels, the daughter of a captain in the U.S. Lighthouse Service on Hatteras Island, was named for Belva Lockwood, one of the first women to run for president, in 1884, the year before Belva Daniels was born. Her husband had been humble and quiet, but Daniels liked her jewelry and finely tailored clothes. She was exacting, stern and tough, including on her children, locking Cora Mae in a closet for punishment and telling her that snakes were coming to get her. Belva Daniels loved to fish. The sun had cooked and drawn tight the skin over her high cheekbones, below her piercing eyes. She was a charter member of Mount Olivet United Methodist Church because of the donations she and her husband made to it, but she rarely attended services. Her husband had tried to get her to go, but she told him, "Take care of your own soul, and I'll take care of mine."

On Wednesday, September 20, she told the agents:

> *I don't know what the problem is between Dr. Edwards and Dotty, but I do know they have been having trouble almost ever since they have been married. On numerous occasions, he has been awful mean to Dotty and beaten her up on several occasions. At one time, she had to be admitted to Albemarle Hospital* [in Elizabeth City]. *On numerous occasions, she has had to leave the house and take her children.*
>
> *Dotty's two children told me that on one occasion that Dr. Edwards had tied their mother to a chair and he had their German Police Dog* [German shepherd] *sit beside the chair and would not allow anyone to untie her. I talked to Dotty about this and she would not say anything about it other than Dr. Edwards was just playing and she did not understand why the kids had told anyone about the incident.*
>
> *Dr. Edwards ran his wife and their children off from their home on September 12. She stayed at her mother's home in Manteo until September 16. Dotty has now returned to their home and is living with Dr. Edwards again.*

The agents must have realized that it had been a brief but incredible interview. For the first time, a member of Dotty's powerful family was talking about Dr. Edwards abusing her, as well as Dotty's reluctance to confront the abuse. If the story from the children was true, Edwards was proficient with cords and knots. That should have been crucial in Brenda's case, one of ligature strangulation.

JUST OVER A WEEK later, the agents talked to Dr. Edwards. On Thursday, September 28, at 11:30 a.m., SBI agents Lenny Wise, Jack Thomas and Dan Gilbert interviewed Edwards at his small office. The location of the interview was questionable. If the agents wanted to unsettle Edwards, to get the whole truth from him, they should have interviewed him on their turf, the Ocean House over on the beach, or at least Cahoon's office—standard procedure for investigators. Instead, they ceded control by interviewing Edwards at the place where he would feel most comfortable and strong, his office. The agents began by asking Edwards about his activities during the hours in which Brenda vanished. The dentist made the following statement:

On Friday, June 30, I had a normal workday here and, as far as I know, I went home and had dinner as usual and went to bed at my regular time, which was about 9 or 9:30 p.m. I have no knowledge of leaving my house that night. On the night of July 1, Saturday night, my wife and I had a few words and I left home and went to the Drafty Tavern and there had a few beers with [a local couple]. *I left the tavern at approximately 11:30 to 11:45 p.m. and went back home. My wife and I had another argument, and she left home after I had gone to bed. I woke up at approximately 1:30 a.m. and she was not in the room. I got up and looked and both cars were in the driveway and I took for granted she left the house on foot. I got up, dressed, and went to the sheriff's department and talked to a deputy sheriff whom I believed to be Will Daniels and told him and the radio dispatcher that my wife had left home and asked that they contact Mrs. Cora Mae Basnight* [Dotty's mother] *and see if she were there. The deputy sheriff said he would contact Mrs. Basnight and if Dotty were not there he would put out an alert to see if she could be located. The deputy told me to go on back home and they would contact me later.*

I went back home and waited about 20 minutes. I didn't receive any call from the sheriff's department, so I went on to bed. I wasn't too concerned because my wife and I had had several arguments on weekends when we both were drinking and she would often leave home and go spend the night with her mother or relatives or friends, but she would always come back home the next day.

I didn't know Brenda Joyce Holland, and I don't know Danny Barber, Rodney Brett or Earl Mirus. I do know the house where they lived, but didn't know at the time who was living there, nor had I been on that road on any night that I can remember, but I have been on this road on several occasions during the daytime, especially on weekends, to go to the trash dump. But to my knowledge, I never saw Brenda Joyce Holland.

I've had two traffic violations and that was the only time I've ever been in court.

The agents, at least in their printed record, never questioned Edwards about the fact that his statement ran counter to that of his neighbors, the Stoutenburgs, or about the domestic violence against his wife that her grandmother had detailed. And they never questioned his wife about his statements concerning the night Brenda vanished.

Dr. Edwards agreed to take a lie detector test. He rode with the agents from his office to the Ocean House, where SBI polygraph operator John Vanderford had been standing by. He gave the dentist the test and then told Wise and his fellow agents that, in his opinion, the results showed "Dr. Edwards had no knowledge of who killed Brenda Joyce Holland, nor did he participate in the wrongful death in any manner."

The next day, Wise got a call from Edwards. He had something else to say and wanted them to come by his office. Once again, the SBI agents went to the office, meeting Edwards in his power spot. Agents Wise, Thomas and Gilbert did the interview. Edwards told them that he'd checked his work records for the Saturday morning after Brenda disappeared, and those records showed he'd seen patients from 8:00 a.m. to noon that day. "I could not have been out drinking and stayed up all night and seen all those patients," he told the agents.

The agents left the office and returned to the Ocean House. Shortly thereafter, they entered this sentence into their confidential file on the case: "After discussion, Dr. Edwards has been eliminated as a suspect."

It was an amazing entry because they rarely wrote in their file that suspects had been eliminated, especially not so early and especially not for major suspects. And it came after an interview in which agents had failed to press the dentist hard on his alibi or other major questions about the case, such as how he'd hurt his back or neck around the time that Brenda vanished, why he had been wearing a body cast and why he'd gotten the prescription for Demerol. They'd also failed to ask him about his attacks on Dotty and proficiency with ropes.

Deputy Will Daniels confirmed that Edwards had reported his wife missing early on the Sunday morning after Brenda vanished. But Edwards had also said that Dotty was at home hours earlier, on Saturday night. That assertion directly contradicted what his reliable neighbors, Ray and Jean Stoutenburg, had told the SBI. The Stoutenburg statements also contradicted Edwards's contention that he had worked that Saturday morning, hours after Brenda disappeared. He could not have done that if he was at his house with his mistress. Edwards could have easily falsified the work records he showed the SBI.

The dentist had passed the polygraph test, but those tests are notoriously unreliable, which is why they are inadmissible in court. Polygraph testing had advanced little since its inception in the early twentieth century and was mainly used as a strategic investigative tool—and an often unreliable one at that. Cahoon himself basically acknowledged that, according to a note in the SBI file on Brenda's case. Blackout drunks free of feelings of guilt and zonked out on Demerol, as Edwards might have been, can sail through the tests.

The SBI never made public its clearing of Edwards as a suspect. Many locals continued to suspect and fear him. Among those was Dotty. Several months after Brenda was killed, she stopped by the Twiford house in Manteo, where Brenda had rented her room. Cora Twiford and Dotty's mother, Cora Mae Basnight, were close friends. Now Dotty had something to say to Twiford about Brenda's killing: "I'm sorry, that should have been me." She provided few other details. Sheriff Cahoon and the SBI agents did not press her for information about her husband. They were still concentrating on Danny Barber. Manteo police chief Ken Whittington Sr. would soon give them, and Dennis Midgett and David Whaley, a gut-punch by cranking up the case against those two suspects.

A "Confession"

In October 1967, the SBI disbanded its five-man team on Brenda's case, pulling them off the Outer Banks. The big push was over, but agents continued to work the case from afar. And the next month, they thought they were close to a breakthrough.

In November 1967, SBI agents Lenny Wise and Jack Thomas paid a call on Danny Barber. On the Thursday after Thanksgiving at 11:20 a.m., they interviewed the Carolina student at a Chapel Hill motel. The agents pressed Barber in the small room, trying as ever, to break him. The agents dryly noted that "there was no change in his story except on this occasion he did state that he took Brenda Holland's blouse off when they were lying in bed."

That was a bombshell. The blouse was not found in Barber's house nor on her body when it was found in the sound nor anywhere else. Why had Barber waited so long to divulge that he took off the blouse? That delay, coupled with the original shift in his story, saying that he had taken Brenda to her rooming house when he had not, gave agents even more reason to believe that Barber killed Brenda. What happened to the blouse? They pressed the suspect on the matter but got nothing more from him. Reluctantly, they ended the interview and let him go.

THE NEW YEAR, 1968, dawned with racial strife and the continued carnage of Vietnam. On March 31, 1968, President Lyndon Baines Johnson, after months of protests of "Hey, Hey, LBJ, how many kids did you kill today?" said that he would not seek reelection. Weeks later, the civil rights leader whom Johnson had sparred with and ultimately worked with on landmark civil rights legislation, Reverend Martin Luther King Jr., was assassinated in Memphis.

The SBI investigators kept on Brenda's case. On Thursday, April 25, 1968, two agents based in the Chapel Hill area, R.D. Emerson and J.L. Bellamy, followed up with a stop by Barber's duplex apartment in Chapel Hill. "He appeared visibly shaken upon being contacted by Agents but nevertheless voluntarily consented to be interviewed," Emerson wrote, adding:

> *Agents had dinner with Barber at the Holiday Inn in Chapel Hill and subsequently proceeded to interview him reference instant* [sic] *investigation. He reiterated the information previously furnished* [sic] *by him to Bureau agents. As the interview progressed, subject Barber advised that he would prefer to telephonically contact his lawyer in Fayetteville before answering additional questions and therefore the interview was terminated at 7:25 p.m. He was again contacted at 10:00 p.m. and 10:30 p.m. at which times he claimed to have been unable to reach his Attorney. Agents informed Barber that they would contact him again in the near future.*

THE INITIAL SBI AGENTS on the case spent much of 1968 chasing down fruitless tips, including one in which a wealthy woman from the small town of Williamston, two hours west of Manteo, told the agents that her husband was a possible suspect. They were at their Nags Head cottage during the hours in which Brenda disappeared, she said, and she and her husband had an argument and he left home. When he came back home late the following morning, she said, he had scratches on and around his face and forehead. He said he cut himself shaving, she said, but she knew that was not true. The agents checked out the husband and ruled him out as a suspect.

Linus Edwards went on with his dental practice. His marriage to Dotty was crumbling under his continued abuse of her and constant talk among islanders that he strangled Brenda. Bill Watson, one of the dentist's two sons-in-law, kept up his clandestine push to convince the SBI that Edwards had probably killed Brenda, dumping her body from his boat. Watson spent hours studying tide charts and writing notes from them that he gave to the SBI. The agents, for the most part, ignored him.

But it was almost like Brenda herself was pushing the investigators on. One night after work early in the summer of 1968, several members of the *Lost Colony* company went to the Pioneer Theater in downtown Manteo to watch a new movie starring Rod Steiger. In one scene, a newspaper headline referred to Brenda's case, along with a photo of her. The *Lost Colony* company members couldn't believe it. When the film ended, they had the longtime owner/operator of the Pioneer, George Creef, wind it back. Sure enough, that was Brenda. The name of the movie was *No Way to Treat a Lady*, in which Steiger played a serial killer.

Later that summer, Ann Holland Earley and Vernon Holland and their two daughters visited Manteo for the first time. The Twifords received them warmly and put them up in the room where Brenda had lived. Ann felt strange being in her little sister's old room and being shown the road on which she had taken her last walk. Ann could not fathom why Brenda would have chosen to walk home alone. Vernon met briefly with Sheriff Cahoon on the case, but there was nothing new. The Twifords made it easier by, among other things, feeding them a luscious meal of fried sea trout.

Cora Gray Twiford and Dick Twiford, Brenda's landlords, welcomed her sisters' visits. *Photo by Kim Holland Thorn.*

As the summer wore on, the public pressure on Cahoon and the SBI agents increased, especially around the one-year anniversary of Brenda's slaying. In July 1968, numerous newspapers ran stories about the case, noting that Danny Barber had not returned to the play that season and that Cahoon and the SBI had yet to charge anyone. Several stories tied the mystery to that of the lost colony. "Will the brutal murder of 19-year-old Brenda Joyce Holland one year ago go down in history as yet another mystery on this isle of mysteries?" the *News & Observer* of Raleigh asked. "Few events, short of the disappearance of the first English colony, have attracted such attention across the state and nation as the Holland murder."

MANTEO POLICE CHIEF KEN Whittington Sr., who read the newspapers as well as he read the tea leaves, had his own ideas on the case.

Whittington was twenty-nine, lean and handsome, and sometimes at odds with the town board. He was a native of rural Halifax County, a three-hour drive inland, who'd arrived in Dare County a decade before. He was ambitious, some said overly so, and clashed with the cautious Cahoon. Cahoon's department shared jurisdiction in Manteo with Whittington's department. But because Brenda's body had been found in the county, Cahoon's department had clear jurisdiction. That didn't stop Whittington from stepping in. He worked the case quietly, without Cahoon's permission, continuously pressing Dennis Midgett, Manteo's unofficial "night watchman," for incriminating evidence against David Whaley. Midgett was just a year younger than Whittington but was mentally handicapped.

Many a night, Whittington would pick up Midgett and ride him around Manteo in his patrol car. Midgett saw a lot in his walks and on car rides. He didn't drive, but friends often picked him up. He'd ride around with them, sharing beer and stories. He liked to talk to those friends, and he usually liked to talk to law officers. But Whittington was pressing him harder than anybody ever had. Usually, Midgett's older brother, Paul, served as his protector and would have told Whittington to back off. But Paul was away that summer, serving in the Coast Guard.

Whittington was working on something big. In late July, he let Manteo mayor S.E. Midgett and members of the town commission in on his secret. Then, on Monday, July 22, officials ambushed Cahoon with it.

Cahoon, a savvy politician with many sources, knew that Whittington was hot-dogging his case, and he didn't like it. Months before, Whittington had told the SBI team that Dennis Midgett had told him that he had overheard suspects Rodney Brett and David Whaley making statements indicating that they had killed Brenda. SBI agents Clyde Fentress and Jack Thomas interviewed Midgett. Midgett basically confirmed the account he had given Whittington, but the story did not check out.

Whittington eliminated Brett as a suspect but kept working. Cahoon didn't know how fast his rival was moving. Whittington was playing Manteo officials against Dare County ones and pulling prosecutors into

Former Manteo police chief Ken Whittington danced across a tabletop to confront photographer Drew Wilson in the Duchess of Dare Restaurant in Manteo in the early 1990s. *Photo by Drew C. Wilson/the* Virginian-Pilot.

the mix. The sheriff, in his office in the courthouse that Monday morning, got a call from District Solicitor Wilton Walker, the elected prosecutor for the area, requesting that Cahoon come to the Manteo Police Department in downtown Manteo that afternoon to discuss the Brenda Holland case. Walker wouldn't give any more details before hanging up. The sheriff must have been exasperated.

At the meeting, Cahoon walked into a cigarette-smoky room to see Solicitor Walker, Chief Whittington, Mayor Midgett and members of the Manteo police commission. One of the town officials greeted all and proudly announced that Chief Whittington had secured a confession in the Brenda Holland case and that a clerk would now read that confession:

> *I, Dennis Midgett, after being advised of my constitutional rights, want to say that David Whaley and myself were riding around the night that Miss Brenda Holland was missing. We saw the girl walking toward Manteo on the Burnside Road.…We were traveling in the same direction. David*

Whaley offered the girl a ride and she refused. At which time David Whaley got out of the car and grabbed the girl and told her to get in the car or he would kill her. The girl screamed and he threw her in the back seat and got in the back seat with her. He ran his hand up her dress and she was fighting him and telling him to stop. David kept right on, and got fresh with the girl, after which David Whaley tied the girl's hands behind her, and tied her feet and said he was going to dump her overboard. During all this time, I asked him to stop, but he would not. I got out of the car and told him I was going for help. David Whaley then got out of the car and stopped me and threatened to shoot me, but I did not see a pistol. David Whaley then drove out to the Scarborough Town Road. All the while, the girl was begging him to carry her home, and I was begging him to let me out. After we passed the House of Joy on the Scarborough Road, David Whaley threw her pocketbook out. He drove out to the highway, turned left, and drove to Fort Raleigh. He drove through the [Lost Colony] theater parking lot and threw a book she had with her out the window of the car. He stopped the car and indecently exposed himself by the car. I tried to untie the girl and run, but he stopped me. He started to the bridge and he threw something out of the car. He stopped the car at the highest point on the bridge.

We had a fight. I hit him in the nose and he hit me in the nose. I went to the main part of the bridge and waited. David Whaley then threw the girl overboard. She was screaming. He then turned the car around on the bridge. I got in the car and he floorboarded it back to Manteo and put me out in front of the sheriff's office. Since then, he has been threatening to shoot me or run me over if I talk. We have been in fights since then.

The clerk finished reading. The room was silent. Chief Whittington and his fellow Manteo officials thought there would be applause. They thought this was the break everyone had been looking for, an end to the tourism black eye they had endured since the body had been found the previous summer. But the applause was muted, at least from Sheriff Cahoon and his supporters.

The "confession" was chilling but confusing because of its references to Brenda's body being thrown "overboard" and its lack of clarity about where Dennis Midgett was during the crucial moments. Parts of the confession just didn't sound like Dennis Midgett. For example, he was quoted as saying Whaley "indecently exposed himself." But those words were beyond Midgett's limited vocabulary. The details about where Brenda's possessions were found had already been widely reported in the press.

Sheriff Cahoon read the room. It wasn't quite like sensing the change in temperatures, clouds, wind and wave currents like he and other locals did to know when a storm, nor'easter or even a hurricane was barreling in, but it was, in its own way, akin. It just required a different sense, a political one. Cahoon first won his office in 1946, when Whittington was in grade school. He knew that Whittington was gunning for his job, enlisting the Manteo power structure for support. And the sheriff was ready.

Cahoon stood up and spoke. "I don't want anything done until I call the SBI," he said, "and I don't understand why Dennis Midgett made this statement after being questioned so many times by people involved in the investigation. I will contact all the agents involved and set up a meeting to check the details in this confession. Chief Whittington, don't pick up David Whaley until these details can be checked out."

THE NEXT AFTERNOON AT 3:30 p.m. in the Manteo courthouse, Cahoon met with Solicitor Walker, Supervising SBI Agent Fentress, Chief Whittington and Agents Lenny Wise and Charlie Ray. They made their plans to check out the statement. Representatives of each law enforcement agency asked that Whittington not talk to anyone about the confession and that he not attempt to arrest Whaley.

Whittington said that he'd have to check this with his town board since all the members knew of the statement and were quite disturbed that the sheriff's department and the SBI did not immediately pick up David Whaley. Cahoon just walked out of the room. He had work to do.

One of the first steps, the following Monday, was a drive of more than an hour to Norfolk, Virginia, to re-interview Heinz Karnitschnig, the Austrian-born pathologist who had done the autopsy on Brenda. The sheriff and Agent Wise made that trip together, once again. Dennis Midgett's "confession" implied that Brenda had not been strangled but rather drowned after Whaley threw her off the bridge. The lawmen asked the pathologist if Brenda could have drowned. No, the pathologist said, she did not drown—she was strangled. The only fluid in her, he said, had been a small amount of brownish liquid that he believed to be beer.

Cahoon and Wise then made arrangements to re-interview Whaley the next day, this time in Greenville, where he was living. The town was a drive of more than two hours west of Manteo. Cahoon; his new deputy,

C.C. Duvall (the former Manteo police chief); Wise; and Supervising SBI Agent Clyde Fentress made the drive and sat down with Whaley in an interview room at the Pitt County Courthouse in Greenville at 2:00 p.m. Whaley had continued to maintain his innocence. He'd felt like his own grandfather had suspected him in the case, and that hurt him.

The lawmen told Whaley that they had received additional information and wanted to recheck where he was around the hours Brenda vanished. Whaley said:

> I don't understand why you all are re-interviewing me. I told you in previous interviews my whereabouts on the night Brenda Joyce Holland was reported missing, and who I was with. I submitted to a polygraph test, have been very cooperative with officers throughout the investigation, and was willing to do anything that you all suggested. My story is the same as I reported to you all when I was first picked up. I don't deny being in the company of Dennis Midgett during that night, riding around in my car, but at no time did I see Brenda Joyce Holland walking on the highway or anywhere else in Manteo that night. You all said you had additional information. I wish you'd let me know what it is.

The officers told Whaley about Midgett's new statement. "Well then," Whaley demanded, "let Dennis Midgett face me with this statement."

Cahoon and company had expected they might need Midgett in Greenville that day, and the sheriff had his deputies back in Manteo keeping an eye on him. After Whaley made his demand, the sheriff called his office and ordered that Midgett be picked up and driven to the Greenville courthouse. A deputy drove in Midgett, arriving in Greenville at 5:30 p.m. that evening. Agents Wise and Fentress interviewed Midgett as Cahoon and Duvall watched. Midgett said:

> Over the past 10 months, I have no idea how many times Chief Whittington has picked me up, ridden me around in his police car, and questioned me about David Whaley and the death of Brenda Holland. On the night of July 22, 1968, Chief Whittington carried me to the police department and I made the statement that David Whaley and me had been riding around on the night that Brenda Holland was missing, and we saw her and David Whaley picked her up and tied her up and tried to rape her and then threw her overboard off Manteo bridge. The reason I made this statement was because Chief Whittington was about to drive me crazy and I had told

him over and over and over that I did not know anything about the Brenda Holland case.

Chief Whittington would not leave me alone. He would come pull me off my job, get me out of my house and question me about the death. Once, me and a girlfriend were drinking one night and Whittington carried me out and interviewed me about the case. I told Chief Whittington I knew nothing about the case. The information I gave in the statement was the general talk around Manteo. All I wanted was for Chief Whittington to leave me alone and quit pestering me about Brenda Holland's death. I knew nothing of this death, and I want you all to know I knew nothing as I stated to you all earlier in the investigation. I want this to be the end of this, and I don't want Chief Whittington to ever say anything else to me about it.

The statement I gave earlier was not true. I am sorry I caused all the embarrassment and extra work. Maybe Chief Whittington will now leave me alone. He told me he would get a lot of publicity and maybe a reward for solving the case.

CAHOON AND THE SBI agents believed Midgett. The only error they caught was Midgett saying he gave his "confession" to Whittington on the night of July 22. He had to have given it earlier, as Manteo town officials read the statement at the meeting on the afternoon of July 22.

Cahoon, with Lenny Wise standing by, called Chief Whittington from Greenville and told him that "the confession" was not true and that Dennis Midgett had no knowledge of what happened to Brenda Joyce Holland. "Dennis Midgett is a person with a very low IQ," Wise wrote in the case file, "and it is [this] writer's opinion that he had no idea of the danger in making this statement."

Sheriff Cahoon and the SBI agents had made their share of stumbles in the case. But they, and Deputy Duvall, stood tall for Dennis Midgett. The case was far from over for them. And it was far from over for Ken Whittington, who would get another shot at it, one to redeem himself—after a suspect made a dramatic exit.

"Something Broke Inside Me"

And now it comes at you—this thing we have to fear far worse than death.
Bit by bit, little by little, this wilderness, this everlasting darkness
of the forest creeps in upon us. The end is savagery.

—*Eleanor Dare in* The Lost Colony *(the original 1937 script)*

It was dusk on Valentine's Day 1971. Dr. Linus Edwards was alone in his Manteo kitchen with his loaded .22-caliber pistol. He looked older than his fifty-four years, his brown hair having gone gray, lines on his face. Lights were twinkling on in the houses all around his in the tony Mother Vineyard neighborhood. Edwards could have looked out the windows of his soundfront home and seen those lights, as well as the lights across the Roanoke Sound, those of Nags Head.

TV reception on the Outer Banks was sketchy. But if the dentist was tuned to one of the three networks that Sunday evening, he might have seen that North Carolina's Richard Petty was on his way to winning the Daytona 500 way down the coast, in Florida. The *Ben-Hur* movie would have its first showing on TV that night.

Edwards didn't care much for those shows or anything else. He just sat there at his kitchen table, scribbling on a notepad, his pistol nearby. January and February were particularly desolate for area residents, with many businesses closed and nothing to do but watch the wind whip up the ocean and sounds. The locals often said that if you could you endure a January and February, it was, at least, a big step toward becoming one of them. Edwards had been through several winters. But few islanders accepted him or thought of him as one of their own. Many believed that he had killed Brenda and gotten away with it.

He could not have cared less that Valentine's night, if he ever had. His last ex-wife, Dotty, was from a strong local clan, but she was done with him, their divorce having become final the year before. She had moved on and taken back her last name of Fry.

So the dentist's house was quiet, had been for some time. Gone was Dotty's laughter and that of her two small children. Gone as well were the loud arguments he had with her. He was alone. His other ex-wife in the area, Ida Edwards, wasn't interested in his talk of reuniting, nor was his ex-mistress.

Edwards just worked and came home and brooded. And he drank. The week before, he went on a bender so bad he finally had his lawyer, Dwight Wheless, drive him to the hospital in Columbia to dry out. Columbia was a small town on the Scuppernong River, a thirty-minute drive west of Manteo, a lonely ride through piney swamps and desolate fish camps. They were an odd couple for the trip. Wheless was thirty, a straight arrow active in the Civil Air Patrol. Edwards was almost a quarter century older, a dissolute drunk. But Wheless was compassionate.

When Edwards was ready for release from the Columbia hospital, Wheless picked him up and drove him home, leaving him there about 3:15 p.m. that Sunday afternoon. The dentist ran at least one errand: he delivered a set of dentures that one of his friends, W.W. Harvey, the town's general practice doctor, had ordered. The Harveys weren't home. The front door was unlocked, as doors often were on the island. Edwards placed the boxed dentures neatly on the Harveys' dining room table and left.

Edwards telephoned Wheless twice that Sunday afternoon. In those two calls, Edwards "seemed perfectly normal," Wheless would later say, discussing plans to reopen his office Monday morning and saying that he had contacted someone to come in and set up appointments for him.

But when Edwards called Wheless a third time, at 6:00 p.m., the lawyer noticed a change in his friend's "voice and attitude." Edwards wanted him to come over. Edwards told Wheless that he had also made calls asking for Dr. Harvey and Sheriff Cahoon to come to his house at the same time. Wheless told Edwards that he would come as soon as he could get his children to bed. His wife was sick with the flu.

Dr. Harvey and his wife were at a Valentine's party, so they missed Edwards's phone call. It's unknown why the sheriff's office didn't respond to his call immediately.

Wheless got to the dentist's house just before 7:00 p.m. Entering through an unlocked door, he found Edwards lying on the kitchen floor, bleeding from a head wound, his pistol nearby. The lawyer called the sheriff's office to request an ambulance, which transported Edwards to the Naval Hospital in Portsmouth, Virginia, a drive of about an hour and a half. The Elizabeth City hospital was closer, but it probably lacked a neurosurgeon. Edwards's shot had knocked him unconscious, but he hung on for two days, finally dying at 5:00 a.m. on February 16, 1971. It was eleven Februarys past the one when his father had died. The son was buried with full military honors at Maplewood Cemetery in his native Durham, beside the father he never understood and who never understood him. Only a few people from Manteo attended. His ex-mistress was among them. Dotty was not.

Edwards had finished what he started with that suicide attempt at the South Carolina army base more than a decade before. And maybe he'd been subconsciously wanting to die before that—and after it. There was the anger at his parents. There was the self-hatred that manifested in his affairs, drinking and violence against others.

His suicide left myriad questions. One of Edwards's relatives said that the change in his demeanor that Sunday afternoon came about because he started drinking beer. But why had this macho man chosen a tiny .22-caliber for his suicide weapon? A larger caliber would have instantly completed the job. He shot himself in the upper left side of his head. That angle would suggest he was left-handed. But when he tried suicide in November 1960, he slit his left wrist. That would suggest he was right-handed. Was he ambidextrous, or was one of the reports wrong?

The biggest question was whether Edwards left a suicide note, perhaps one in which he'd confessed to Brenda's slaying. Wheless told SBI agent Lenny Wise that there was none. "There was a notepad on the table in the kitchen, in the room in which Dr. Edwards was lying on the floor, and there were some figures on this pad, but there was no note left by Dr. Edwards," Wheless said. "I was his attorney and had all of his papers, and there was no suicide note in any of the papers. I have no idea who might have put the word out that Dr. Edwards left a suicide note, but it wasn't true."

David Payne, the teenage *Lost Colony* worker whom Brenda had taught to swim, would later tell Brenda's sister Kim that his parents always told him that Edwards left two notes—one to the sheriff and one to Dr. Harvey. Wise wrote in the file that he and Cahoon believed that the information about the suicide note was put out by one of Edwards's sons in law, Bill Watson, "due to his dislike for Dr. Edwards." Many potential witnesses hate the people they're trying to bring to justice. Watson had hounded Cahoon and the SBI agents, but many of his reports had been credible.

In a November 30, 1971 report in the SBI file following up on Edwards's suicide, Supervising Agent Clyde Fentress briefly but sloppily outlined the mistaken identity theory. He wrote that Dotty was "6 or 7 inches taller than Brenda Holland was," when the actual height difference was only about four inches. (Dotty was five feet, eleven inches tall and Brenda was five feet, seven inches tall.) He wrote that Edwards was driving a Jeep on the night Brenda vanished, when he'd actually been driving his Ford Fairlane and didn't own a Jeep. Fentress concluded, "At this time and for sometime [*sic*], Dr. Edwards has been eliminated as a suspect in this case."

Why hadn't the sheriff's office responded to Edwards's call? Why had the dentist wanted his lawyer, his doctor and his sheriff to come? Was he going to confess that he killed Brenda to them? Or was he going to deny it once again?

As soon as the ambulance lit up the winter night speeding up Mother Vineyard Road to Edwards's house, the rumors started, spilling out of that neighborhood and across the island. Many islanders would continue to believe that there had been a confession note and that officials were lying when they said there was none. A few locals even suspected that Edwards had been murdered and the sheriff's office covered up the crime, despite the lack of any evidence to support that claim.

This much was certain: The investigation of Brenda's slaying had fizzled even before Edwards took his life. Cahoon and the SBI agents had continued to concentrate on Danny Barber, but they were getting nowhere and doing nothing beyond periodic updates on his whereabouts after he'd graduated from Carolina. After Edwards committed suicide, investigators let the case die.

But Cahoon continued to dismiss Edwards as a suspect. Sometime after the dentist killed himself, the sheriff saw a friend in downtown Manteo and called him over to his cruiser. The friend was Joseph L.S. Terrell, who'd written a story on Brenda's case for *Startling Detective* magazine. The sheriff pulled a pistol from underneath his car seat and said it was the gun Edwards killed himself with. Cahoon looked Terrell in the eye and said, "That man didn't anymore kill that girl than you or I did."

By then, Cahoon had moved into Edwards's old neighborhood, Mother Vineyard. In response to Brenda's slaying, the Roanoke Island Historical Association built the Morrison Grove apartments near the theater to provide safer housing for members. Downtown Manteo lost the vibrancy of the theater folks carousing when they got off work.

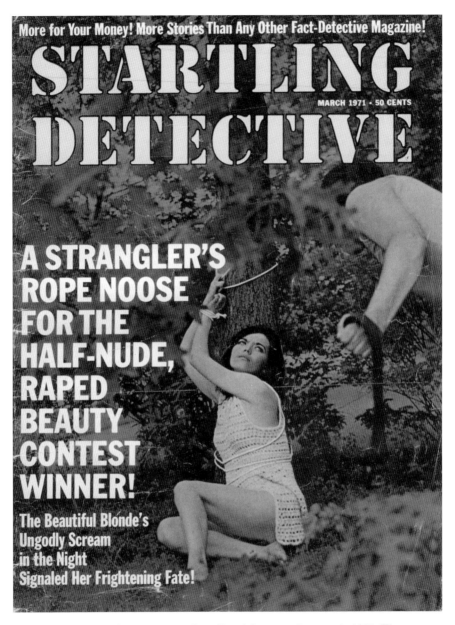

Startling Detective magazine put a story about Brenda's case on its cover in 1971. The story by Joseph L.S. Terrell, a responsible journalist, was factual and meant to generate new tips about the case, but Brenda's family did not like the cover. *Courtesy Kim Holland Thorn.*

THE JUNE AFTER EDWARDS killed himself, one of his fellow suspects, David Whaley, who also came from Durham to Mother Vineyard, married a pretty young woman in her hometown of Wilson, a few hours inland from Manteo. Reverend Kenneth Whitney, Whaley's grandfather, co-led the 5:00 p.m. ceremony at Grace Baptist Church. Whaley, standing by candles at the front of the church, smiled as his bride, escorted by her father, walked down the aisle. She wore a gown of white chiffon and carried a bouquet of white mums with an orchid. A woman sang "There's a Time for Us," a hit from a Hollywood version of *Romeo and Juliet* that came out in the fall of 1968. Lines of the song resonated:

> *A time for us, someday there'll be*
> *When chains are torn by courage born of a love that's free.*

A few months before the *Romeo and Juliet* movie came out, Manteo police chief Ken Whittington had tried in vain to pin Brenda's slaying on Whaley. That seemed far in the past on the day of the wedding. Whaley was twenty-three. He'd resumed his studies at East Carolina University. His wife was a graduate of the school and taught special education. The song from the movie ended with a line about "A new world, a world of shining hope for you and me."

By the following September, Whaley was dead. His family kept the details close. An obituary published in the *Coastland Times* said that he died after a "critical illness" of three months and requested that donations be made to a cancer fund. His funeral was held in St. Joseph's Episcopal Church in Durham. He was buried at Maplewood Cemetery in that city, not far from Dr. Edwards in the same graveyard. Both men had been returned to the city they had fled years before.

MORE YEARS PASSED. In the early 1980s, C.C. Duvall, the Manteo police chief who had Brenda's clothes washed before they were sent to the FBI for testing, apparently at Sheriff Cahoon's request, was convicted of accessory after the fact to a 1979 hit-and-run that resulted in the death of eighty-seven-year-old Cloice Creef of Manteo, a former caretaker of the courthouse. At the time of the crime, Duvall was one of Cahoon's top deputies. Following a controversial trial, Duvall was convicted of helping to cover up the hit-and-run. He did one year in state prison. He would redeem himself in the years to come.

In May 1982, Bill Watson, the son-in-law of Edwards who had tried to implicate him in Brenda's slaying, made a return visit to his hometown of Ballinger, Texas. He had been living in Colorado, working construction jobs. On the return visit to his hometown, Watson stepped out between parked cars and was hit by another car, sustaining fatal head injuries.

Cahoon kept telling Brenda's parents that Danny Barber was the killer, but there wasn't enough evidence to charge him. SBI agent Lenny Wise backed the sheriff. Wise was usually unflappable. But once, when an islander friend pressed him, contending that Barber was not Brenda's slayer, Wise blew up, telling her that he couldn't tell her all he knew but that Barber was the killer.

Barber, by then known as "Dan" instead of "Danny," was rising through the executive ranks at Sara Lee Hosiery, having started with the company in 1970 at its headquarters in Winston-Salem, in central North Carolina, and then taking posts around the country. He once talked privately about being a suspect in Brenda's killing. He talked about how vulnerable, alone and helpless he felt as the SBI agents grilled him for hours in a hot room at Cahoon's office in Manteo, not being able to convince them that he was not the killer, and how grateful he was to one of his brothers for retaining an attorney who ended the initial interrogations. He did not go into details but did say that he could not understand why anyone would kill Brenda. As he tried to make sense of what happened, he offered a theory: Months before that summer, he'd been in a serious relationship with a woman from New York City. Barber and the woman broke up, but he continued to be friends with her, sometimes talking to her in phone chats. By then, he said, his ex-girlfriend was dating a man involved in organized crime. That man was jealous of Barber's friendship with his girlfriend. Barber wondered if that man contracted Brenda's strangling to frame him. He never shared that theory with investigators.

Barber talked fondly of his three *Lost Colony* seasons. He vacationed on the Outer Banks and took in the play. Barber did not announce his presence at the Waterside Theater, preferring to move in and out quietly.

During those years, Gerri Holland said her daughter came to her in a dream. Brenda started to name her killer. Then she vanished.

Brenda's sister Kim never really felt the full impact of the loss until she was thirteen—four years after the killing—and a boy was visiting her at her Canton home. Kim was showing him photos of her family when she came on one of Brenda. She suddenly realized for the first time that her sister really was gone forever. She burst into tears and couldn't stop. Years later, Kim wrote in a personal narrative of the case that her parents never really recovered:

> *Mom found her best therapy was to go to work and stay busy. Dad, he continued to work at the mill, but he also continued to drink, more and more, and smoke lots of cigarettes, one right after the other. Dad had always had a problem with alcohol which we attributed to his being in the war, but Mom knew this was how he was handling the loss of Brenda. The phone calls from the sheriff grew very infrequent.*

Gerri Holland often accidentally called Kim "Brenda." She idolized her lost daughter, endlessly talking about what a good Christian girl she was, one who had no faults. She monitored Kim's every move, worried that a murderer would take her away as well. Kim didn't apply for a four-year college, knowing that her mother couldn't stand to have another child leave.

Kim's brother, Charles, was crushed as well. "Something broke inside me when she was killed," he said years later. "After that, I hate to say it, I just didn't care."

On a snowy evening a few years after Brenda was killed, the family fissure broke wide open. Gerri Holland needed a battery replaced in her car to get to work the next morning. Shotgun Holland, drunk, had the battery but wouldn't put it in. Charles Hoyt was fifteen. He confronted his father in their backyard, the rage at losing Brenda and his parents' inadequacy in the face of it welling up. He swung at Shotgun, the start of an epic fistfight that ended with Charles on top of his father, pounding his leathery face bloody until Gerri came screaming out of the house and Kim hit Charles with a broomstick to save Shotgun. They rose, covered with mud and snow, and trudged inside. Charles apologized to his father. Shotgun waved it off. "You're a man now," he said. "You're not a kid. I had to do the same thing with my dad."

The Holland children were not alone in their darkness. At the other end of the state, Dr. Edwards's ex-stepdaughter, Claudia Fry Sluder Harrington, was haunted by the five years her mother had spent married to Edwards.

Part III

THE RECKONING

MANTEO, NORTH CAROLINA
1979–2018

"He Came Looking for Me and Found Her"

It's 2:00 p.m. on Wednesday, June 13, 2018, in a small hot room in the Dare County Sheriff's Office. I am sitting in on an interview that Tony Cummings, part of the State Bureau of Investigation's cold-case unit, is conducting with Claudia Fry Sluder Harrington, the daughter of Dr. Linus Edwards's ex-wife, Dotty Fry. They're talking about Brenda, but they might just as well be talking about one of the vanished colonists of 1587. Welcome to parallel island time, where loss and mystery are part of life. Nothing is ever really buried on these sands where storms unearth the ribs of ships sunk hundreds of years before. Tourists drown all the time on the nearby beaches, and storm-hardened commercial fishermen sometimes perish on mean shoals, ranging from ones close to home to those far away. Brenda's death was different. "We had more brutal murders in Dare County," Sheriff Frank Cahoon once said, "But this one was about a sweet, innocent person—a Miss Congeniality—who had come here to be in the show."

We were in that interview room because my freelance investigative columns in the *Coastland Times* that spring and summer of 2018 had led the SBI to reopen Brenda's case. I had a good foundation on which to build: In 1986, Dotty Fry had finally talked publicly about the case. She said that Dr. Edwards, before they divorced in 1970, repeatedly confessed to her that he killed Brenda. Besides having unique knowledge of the case, Dotty was the elected register of deeds for Dare County. One of her brothers, Marc Basnight, was a state senator and would later become one of the most powerful Senate heads in North Carolina history.

Cahoon had retired by then. The SBI said little about Dotty's statement and did even less.

For my first column on the case, I tracked down one of Brenda's sisters, Kim Holland Thorn, and got comments from her for the column. I quoted her on her belief that Edwards was the killer, as well as Dotty having told her that when Kim visited Manteo in the mid-1990s.

I called Dotty, who still lived in Manteo:

> *"Hello."*
>
> *"Hey, Mrs. Fry. I'm John Railey, a journalist working with the* Coastland Times. *I met you a few times when I lived at Nags Head in the mid-1980s. We had some mutual friends."*
>
> *"Oh yes."*
>
> *"Anyway, what I'm calling about today is the* Lost Colony *murder case of 1967."*
>
> *"Oh yes. I was in* The Lost Colony.*"*
>
> *"Yes ma'am, I wanted to ask you about what you said several years ago, that your ex-husband, the dentist, killed Brenda Holland."*
>
> *"I was married three times, but I was never with a dentist."*
>
> *"Yes, ma'am, but…"*

Dotty hung up on me. She was only eighty-five, but she was old beyond her years. That conversation led to an alliance with Dotty's daughter, Claudia, and Kim Thorn to find out who killed Brenda. A source gave me a copy of the SBI's classified file on Brenda's case. It was the Holy Grail, detailing the twists, turns and failures in the case that had never been made public. Using the file as a start, I tracked down case insiders and interviewed them for my columns, prompting the SBI to reopen its probe.

I HAD GROWN UP with the case, spending summers at my family's place nestled against a high oceanfront dune in Nags Head. It was a flat-topped cottage of cement painted the same shade of turquoise as the best Bahamian waters. My parents, riding the post–World War II boom, bought it with a partner for about $14,000 in 1961. My father had served on an LST in the U.S. Navy in the South Pacific, ferrying marines into battles on remote islands held by the Japanese. One of his fellow officers on the ship was Billy Tarkington, a good man from Manteo who became one of my father's best friends. He was in my parents' wedding and led them to Nags Head.

Billy, whom we children called "Uncle Billy," visited our cottage often and made us feel like locals, telling us the inside stories of Manteo and the beach. We'd visit him at his motel, the Ocean House. Our parents would talk with Uncle Billy in the office as we children played in the pool. We'd take breaks in the air-conditioned chill of the office and listen to the adults chat. In the summer of 1967, I remember Uncle Billy showing me the 1967 *Lost Colony* program, pointing out Brenda's photo and saying that she'd recently been killed and her body was found in the Albemarle Sound. Then he turned a few pages forward and showed me a photo of Danny Barber, whom he said probably killed her. I got a chill down my back, envisioning that pretty girl floating dead in the sound and hating Barber. I was six years old that summer of 1967, constantly wondering at the adult world. There was the wildness of the Casino, the nightclub that my older siblings went to. And there was that photo of Brenda that haunted me.

As I dove into Brenda's story in the spring of 2018, I realized why Uncle Billy thought Danny Barber killed Brenda: Sheriff Cahoon and Uncle Billy, related by marriage, were good friends and owned the Ocean House together. The motel was headquarters for the SBI agents working on Brenda's case. When Uncle Billy showed me the program that summer, the agents were probably quietly working in their nearby rooms.

My father knew Cahoon through Uncle Billy. Working at the Seafare restaurant in Nags Head during summers when I was college, all I knew about Cahoon was that he was a looming law-and-order presence to be feared. He was the stern man in the photos in the *Coastland Times*, near the court report that detailed the travails of the souls Cahoon and his men had arrested for a variety of charges, including the one I and so many others dodged: drunk driving. As I became obsessed with Brenda's case, I began to wonder if Cahoon might have gotten this one wrong, as guilty as I felt about questioning this good friend of my Uncle Billy.

AS MY COLUMNS RAN in the *Coastland Times* with my e-mail address at the bottom, I got some tips that helped. One of the best came from Marilyn Whittington, the widow of former Manteo police chief Ken Whittington Sr. She e-mailed me a PDF of her husband's handwritten notes from 1979, in which he said that Dotty told him that year that she had tried in vain to talk to Sheriff Cahoon and SBI agent Lenny Wise about her belief that her husband killed Brenda. That was a groundbreaking revelation, especially coming from Whittington.

He was the chief who, in July 1968, had clashed with Sheriff Cahoon over Brenda's case. Whittington had pressed Dennis Midgett of Manteo, who was mentally challenged, into making a statement implicating David Edward Whaley in Brenda's killing. Cahoon and the SBI agents had seen the huge holes in the statement and squelched it.

It was a blow for Whittington. He stayed in his job for a few more years, occasionally clashing with the town board, until he resigned in June 1974, saying that he needed more pay to support his family. In the years after, he worked in building restoration and renovation, as well as in private investigation. On his own time, he continued to explore Brenda's case. In cursive notes on a yellow legal pad dated January 4, 1979, he conveyed his thoughts:

> *I decided that all these years everyone had worked on Danny Barber and David Whaley and come up with nothing but questions. I decided to talk with Dr. Edwards' wife Dotty. I told her that I had thought about looking into this case again and she said it was a good idea. She was glad somebody was. She said that no one had questioned her about it and she had tried on several occasions to talk to Sheriff Cahoon and SBI Agent Lenny Wise but they acted like they were not interested, that they were almost certain Danny Barber was guilty. I've always thought David Whaley was guilty, and maybe all of us had been looking in the wrong direction.*
>
> *After talking with Dotty for about one-and-a-half hours, the circumstantial evidence was overwhelming. She said that the night that the girl was missing, she and Dr. Edwards had a very bad quarrel and he threatened to kill her. Dr. Stoutenburg was a witness. He heard Dr. Edwards threaten her.*

Whittington detailed that Dotty fled, that Edwards was riding around looking for her, that he knew she had a friend who lived in Barber's house and that he may have come upon Brenda. He may have killed her in a case of mistaken identity.

The new part that Whittington brought to the case were Dotty's words about the lack of interest from Agent Wise and Sheriff Cahoon, as well as Dotty's interest in reopening the case and her possible willingness to go public. It's unknown if Whittington tried to approach the sheriff and the SBI with his findings. Given that Cahoon and Whittington were never close and had fallen out over the Whaley angle in 1968, and that Cahoon had never been very interested in the Edwards angle, it's doubtful that Whittington would have gotten anywhere if he had approached the sheriff.

In 1985, crusading journalist Ray Py took on the case in investigative stories for the *Outer Banks Current*. One of his main sources was Whittington. In December 1985, Py told the SBI in phone conversations that it should talk to Dotty and Whittington. The following spring, agents finally interviewed Dotty, for the first time in the nineteen-year history of the case.

On April 7, 1986, at 12:20 p.m., SBI agents W.M. Thomas, W.A. "Doc" Hoggard and Ken Bazemore interviewed Dotty in her office at the Dare County Courthouse. Hoggard, who lived in Dare County and knew Dotty, introduced the other agents to her. He was a graduate of Brenda's school, Campbell College. He was there after her and never met her.

Dotty was fifty-three, as charming and lively as ever, as arresting in her good looks as ever, in a blouse and skirt that day. She greeted the agents in her brogue. She sat back in her chair, crossed her long legs and lit up one of her Virginia Slim cigarettes. She had always been comfortable talking with men, especially about her island. This was her sand. She was now an elected official, years past the days when Edwards had oppressed her. He'd been dead for more than fifteen years. What was left of him was rotting away in a graveyard, back in his Durham hometown. Dotty smiled and, one by one, made eye contact with each of the three agents. She made small talk with them about Manteo, laughing at points, her ocean-blue eyes twinkling. Then, because they had finally asked, she did what she'd never done before: she told lawmen about the hours when Brenda was killed. She didn't hesitate much, other than to take an occasional long drag on her cigarette and flick the ashes in a tray. She took the agents back to the summer of 1967. It soon became obvious that she didn't think much of her ex, Linus Edwards. But in a peculiar twist, maybe a reflection of the power he once held over her, she referred to him as "Dr. Edwards," never as "Linus" or "Edwards."

She told the agents that Dr. Edwards was the main suspect. When they were married, she said, they were prone to have weekends or several days of heavy intoxication. He had assaulted her numerous times, she said. At the time Brenda was killed, Dotty said, she and Dr. Edwards had a violent argument and she fled their house. Dotty continued:

> *I feel that because of Dr. Edwards' insanely intoxicated condition, he continued to look for me all night. I feel like, from the state of mind he was*

in, that he possibly met Brenda Joyce Holland walking back to her house, and due to the physical similarities between us, he mistakenly picked her up and strangled her…

Dr. Edwards demanded my loyalty and would not hesitate to assault me if I did not comply with his demands. I feel like, because of the friendship of Sheriff Cahoon and Dr. Edwards, the investigation was not very thorough. When he was very drunk, Dr. Edwards would claim that he had murdered Brenda Holland.…I wish that all suspicions of Brenda Holland's boyfriend, Danny Barber, could be removed. In my mind, I sincerely believe that Dr. Edwards was the main suspect.

Barber wasn't Brenda's boyfriend; they were just dating. Otherwise, the brief interview was a nor'easter. Edwards had confessed to killing Brenda. And Dotty said that the sheriff was lax in his investigation of Edwards because they were friends. The interview could have gone on for hours, but the agents soon ended it. They did not ask Dotty to elaborate.

The SBI did not go public with Dotty's revelation. But Dotty, having broken her silence, was not done. She confirmed to Ray Py that she talked to the SBI. And in a story by Py that was published in the *Carolina Coast*, a tabloid of the *Virginian-Pilot* newspaper of Norfolk, Virginia, on August 7, 1986, she elaborated. She said this of Edwards: "When he became angry, or drank too much, he would tell me he did it [killed Brenda.] Then later he would deny it."

Dotty confirmed the mistaken identity theory:

I was in the same neighborhood as Holland and I think he came looking for me and found her. We were about the same height and had about the same color of hair. She was younger than me but the street was very dark. When I came home, my husband was already there, and when he saw me, he turned white as a sheet of paper.…Dr. Edwards was very intelligent, very strong, and very abusive to me when he drank. I was married to him for five years and it was a very bad time. When he died he left no note and no one could understand why he shot himself. It was a long time ago but I think about it quite a lot.…It is all circumstantial about Dr. Edwards, but I have always felt in my heart that he was responsible.

Cahoon, who'd retired in 1982 and was seventy-nine, also talked to Py for the story, implicitly sticking to his contention that Danny Barber was the killer, revealing more about his theory on that than he had before publicly. Cahoon said he believed that Brenda died of suffocation from a pillow or a blanket. Marks found on her neck, Cahoon said, came from the necklace she wore.

The medical examiner had clearly said that Brenda died of ligature strangulation, not suffocation. Cahoon himself had double-checked the cause of death back in 1968 when Chief Whittington had extracted the "confession" from Dennis Midgett against David Whaley, a confession that implied that Brenda drowned after Whaley threw her off the Manns Harbor bridge after Whaley sexually assaulted her and beat her. Back then, when Cahoon and SBI agent Lenny Wise drove to Norfolk, Virginia, to follow up on that statement, the pathologist had reiterated that the cause of Brenda's death was not drowning but rather ligature strangulation, far different from suffocation. The pathologist basically said that the marks on Brenda's neck came from a narrow rope, not a much thinner necklace strand. And if the necklace was so important, why had the investigators given it to Brenda's family the day her body was found, instead of preserving it as evidence?

Whittington had wrongly pressed Dennis Midgett, but Whittington had gotten one thing right. By seriously exploring the Edwards angle all those years later, he was the only initial lawman on the case who got off his long-held theory and explored a new one.

Many locals believed Dotty, that Edwards was the killer. Edwards had once even told Dotty that *she* was the reason Brenda was strangled. If she hadn't run away from him that night, he told her, the killing wouldn't have happened, Edwards's next-door neighbor, attorney Emma Lee Crumpacker, once told a relative.

Other locals wondered why Dotty waited so long to come forward, especially after Edwards killed himself and she no longer had to fear him. But the fact that she spoke out was still courageous. On their small island, she frequently ran into Cahoon. They shared mutual friends. The islanders tend to protect one another, to keep their silence, especially in matters that can bring on the scrutiny of outsiders.

The investigators never told Brenda's parents about the interview with Dotty. From July 1967 on, all they'd ever heard from Sheriff Cahoon, in sporadic phone calls, was that Danny Barber was the killer. Shotgun Holland had lived with that information and obsessed over it as he talked of killing Barber. Then came word from the beach that this woman was saying that the killer was really her ex-husband. The Hollands just happened to hear about it from a relative who discovered the 1986 story after picking up the

Virginian-Pilot while passing through Manteo. Brenda's sister Kim wrote in her personal narrative in 2008:

> *There was a story from a lady who claimed that she was convinced that her now-deceased husband had killed Brenda, mistakenly, because he actually wanted to kill her, his wife. Now mind you, this lady was telling this 19 years after Brenda's murder. My mom was livid, she could not understand how anyone could have kept this to herself all these years. I remember saying, "Mom, if you can believe this story, then justice has been done, this man committed suicide, and you know God says that if a person commits suicide they will burn in hell, so he got what he deserved."*

But neither Kim nor the rest of her family really felt like justice had been done.

In 1995, Deputy R.D. "Buddy" Tillett took his own look at Brenda's case. His entrance was mystical. Buddy is short and charismatically coiled, with a quick smile and light storytelling style that belies his tenacity. In that sense, he is like a latter-day version of Shotgun Holland, Brenda's father. Buddy is evangelical, a believer in signs from on high. He had grown up in Dare County and had long been intrigued by Brenda's slaying, which happened when he was a toddler. As a Dare County deputy, he'd been reading Ben Haas's 1973 novel *Daisy Canfield*, loosely based on the case, in his feed store in downtown Manteo that he ran on the side when a woman walked up. She asked him about the book and said that he should call Brenda's mother. The woman, who never gave Buddy her name, gave him the unlisted number for Gerri Holland. He called her. She told him she had been praying that, before she died, she would find out who killed her daughter. Buddy told her that he couldn't make any promises he couldn't keep, but he'd do his best. He successfully pushed his superiors for the right to take a fresh look at the case and secured access to the SBI file.

Soon thereafter, Kim made her first trip to Roanoke Island. She wrote:

> *When we arrived in Manteo, it was very hard on me. Really difficult coming across the sound, because I knew that was the water where Brenda was thrown in and her body was found. I remembered some of the things that I had heard as a child about the investigation, so it was like a movie in my mind. All the questions we all asked and wondered about I was now experiencing. I imagined being Brenda on this date, deciding to walk back, seeing myself on this long road she supposedly started walking on, back toward town. This visit was quite overwhelming. Deputy Tillett*

Kim Holland Thorn (*left*) and Dotty Fry during Kim's 1995 visit to the island. *Courtesy Kim Holland Thorn.*

met us and we talked a lot, or listened a lot. He had several places to take us, and people he wanted us to meet.

One of those people was Dotty. Kim continued:

Dotty Fry worked at the courthouse, so we went there, of all places. Now, remember, this is a clannish town, it didn't take long for people to realize who you are and what you are doing in their town, and we're going to talk with this lady at the courthouse. So we did, and Dotty explained that even though she was a few years older than Brenda they actually resembled each other, people had mentioned that the looked a lot alike. They both had short, bleached blond hair and were about the same size. I can buy the resemblance due to the hair thing. She said that her husband was the town dentist, so that made him like automatically superior, but he was a drunk. An abusive, wife-beating drunk and that, although he had been drunk a lot and threatened her a lot, she knew that this one particular night he was going to kill her if he got his hands on her. So she fled…

She said everyone that was local was extremely hush-hush about the whole incident. People were scared. Dotty did tell us that, even though the town was accustomed to the ever-changing cast and employees of the Colony, Brenda was different. Everyone who met her liked her. And she fit in. Dotty said the reason she spoke out in the story many years later was conscience, and that was the only way to explain what she thought had happened....Of course, it was enlightening to hear her story, especially in person. I believed it the first time I read it, and I totally believed her story after she told me in person.

Buddy had started by studying the case file, deciding that it was too easy to put the killing on Dr. Edwards. He did new interviews. He interviewed Dotty and nailed down her story about the night Brenda was killed and Edwards's confession to Dotty that he had killed her. He interviewed Dr. Stoutenburg, who confirmed what he'd told the SBI about Edwards threatening Dotty on the night Brenda vanished. Buddy covered the Danny Barber angle. By phone from his Manteo office, Buddy interviewed Barber in his Winston-Salem home. Barber, who maintained his innocence, was open and receptive, offering to help in any way he could.

Most important was a hit Buddy scored by pure luck. On patrol one night, he responded to a call at Harry Niser Sr.'s house outside Manteo. Niser, a construction worker, told Tillett that Edwards had confessed the killing to him. He swore Buddy to secrecy. Buddy honored that and only revealed the story to me after Niser had died. Buddy ruled out the other suspects and, against his initial intuition, began to concentrate on Edwards. He interviewed Dr. Harvey, the island doctor who had examined Brenda's body right after it was found. Harvey told Buddy that he was on the right track in concentrating on Edwards.

A few years after reopening the case, Buddy left the department for another job. His investigation told him that Edwards was the killer. Despite Buddy's hard work, no one else in local law enforcement circles showed much interest in the case.

Dotty spoke out once more, in 1997, telling Sarah Avery of the *News & Observer* of Raleigh that Edwards had confessed to her that he had killed Brenda. Shotgun Holland never bought that. He kept believing that Danny Barber did it. He'd sit in his daddy's rocking chair in the basement of his Canton home, smoking Kool cigarettes, drinking and stewing in his fury at Barber. "I just ought to go down there and finish what I should have," he'd say.

Dare County deputy Buddy Tillett, who re-opened the case in 1995. Former Manteo police chief Ken Whittington is in the background. *Courtesy Kim Holland Thorn.*

In the late 1990s, Holland had a cerebral stroke and fell into dementia. "I looked in his eyes and saw the father I knew disappear," Charles Holland said. His father's mind, he said, became stuck in the 1940s, often talking as if he was back in that time. He was finally free of the pain of losing Brenda. He died on September 1, 2003.

Gerri Holland came to believe that Edwards was the killer. She was angry at Cahoon for never charging him. In declining health, she descended from her mountains to spend her last years with Kim in southeastern North Carolina in the small town of Vanceboro. She lived in a guest cottage on Kim's property, surrounded by what her slain daughter had left behind: Brenda's letters to her, condolence letters to the family, Brenda's high school yearbooks and her photos. Gerri kept a framed photo of Brenda by her bed. There was another artifact in the room: the 1967 calendar Brenda had carried with her to the coast. On the June page, Gerri had scrawled, "Manteo, the worst place on earth."

Gerri died on June 14, 2013. Shotgun and Gerri Holland are buried by Brenda in their family plot outside Canton.

DOTTY ON THE BRIDGE

During the summer of 2018, I kept believing that the cold-case agent, Tony Cummings, would finally do what no other lawman had been able to: crack Brenda's case. He was a retired SBI agent who worked cold cases on a contract basis for the agency. He was a respected officer who'd had some measure of success at solving these cases. His work depended on physical evidence.

As Cummings searched for that evidence in Brenda's case, Brenda's sister Kim and Dotty's daughter, Claudia Harrington, got to know each other through me. They share a love for dogs, underdogs in general, and a hatred of injustice. They are cousins in trauma if not in blood, Claudia having been seven and living in Edwards's house in Manteo in that summer of 1967 and Kim having been nine up in the mountains when Brenda was killed. Kim had graduated from Haywood County Community College up in her mountains. She has a son, Ben.

Claudia is Manteo through and through. As a child, she hung out backstage at *The Lost Colony* with her grandmother Cora Mae Basnight, who played the Indian character Agona, and Renie Rains, the costumer for the play who was Brenda's boss. Claudia spent a lot of time with her grandmother, a soothing influence during the Edwards years and after. She graduated from the University of North Carolina–Chapel Hill and raised two sons, Barron and Bodan.

By the summer of 2018, the legends of the town at the time of Brenda's slaying—Sheriff Frank Cahoon, Renie Rains, Cora Mae Basnight, Joe

Layton and Andy Griffith—were all dead. So were most of the players in the case, including Robert Midgett and former Manteo police chief Ken Whittington. The *Lost Colony* play was still thriving, drawing in the tourists. Through careful planning, the town had retained and refined its original character, the present living with the past. By the 1970s, Manteo had renamed many of its downtown streets for historical figures, such as Sir Walter Raleigh and Ananias Dare, and fictional characters from *The Lost Colony*, such as Agona. Standing on a short bridge over Dough's Creek named for Cora Mae, who made the role of Agona her own, you can look over at the *Elizabeth II*, a re-creation of the ship the colonists who would be lost came in on.

The house where Danny Barber lived that summer on Burnside Road still stood in 2018, as did the frame house just up the road where lived Robert Midgett, who heard the "ungodly scream" that night. Just across U.S. 64, not a half mile away, was the house where Brenda rented her room from the Twifords. The houses hadn't changed much since 1967. The other artifact from that time that still stands is the old bridge over the Croatan Sound from Manteo to Manns Harbor. Traffic on the bridge is light. You can drive to the highest point, forty-five feet over the Croatan Sound, and stop. Many islanders believe that the killer tossed Brenda's body from that point.

Some of them say that the killer was David Whaley, the party boy who lived in Mother Vineyard. My host from the prologue said that he heard Whaley's beat-up motorboat going out into the Roanoke Sound the night Brenda vanished. Was Whaley headed out to dump Brenda's body? There is no mention of that in the SBI file. The mentally challenged man whom Manteo police chief Ken Whittington pressured into implicating Whaley, Dennis Midgett, said that Whaley used his car to dump Brenda's body off the bridge. He never mentioned a boat. Then Midgett recanted the whole statement. Dennis Midgett had died several years before. But his older brother, Paul Midgett of Manteo, told me in the summer of 2018 that Whittington was looking for a scapegoat. "You didn't have to be an Einstein to work for the Manteo Police Department then," he said.

My host was sure of this: Danny Barber, the man who taught him to slalom water-ski all those years ago, did not kill Brenda. In 1994, in Winston-Salem, Barber had retired from his position of vice-president of national sales for Sara Lee Hosiery. He often vacationed on the Outer Banks, but he never looked up old friends or acquaintances there. He died on January 15, 2011, at the age of sixty-eight. In his obituary photo, Barber is chunky and gray-haired, happy, wearing glasses and sporting a mustache.

The other key players in the case, including Lenny Wise and C.C. Duvall, the Manteo police chief who had Brenda's clothes washed and became one of Cahoon's top deputies, were dead as well. Duvall left his criminal conviction behind and redeemed himself as Dare County's chief helicopter pilot for its air ambulance service. In 1989, as he and medical technician Stephenie G. Willoughby were headed back to Dare after delivering a patient to a Norfolk hospital, they were killed when the copter Duvall was piloting crashed at night into an unlit radio tower under construction at the Currituck County town of Coinjock. Centel Cellular Telephone Company did not admit any liability but agreed to pay $1 million to the federal government and do a two-year safety awareness campaign in its industry on antennae marking and lighting. Duvall was fifty-three and Willoughby was thirty-four. They were widely mourned as heroes. The county's copter is now housed in a hangar named for them.

The departed cast also included one-time suspects John Davis Scarborough, John Langston Daniels and Rodney Brett. Brett had moved to Norfolk, where he worked in an antique store. He died in the winter of 2018. He was seventy-nine.

Barber's other housemate, Earl Mirus, is still alive. He knew Dotty as a bit of a flirt, he told me, but he never had an affair with her, as Edwards thought. Mirus said that he was too in love with his girlfriend at the time for that.

Buddy Tillett left the island for a security officer job in New Hampshire but had returned by 2018 to respond to the death of a son and to care for a sick relative. He was initially reluctant to talk publicly about Brenda's case, saying that many of his fellow locals just wanted to bury it. He was worried that speaking out might hurt his job prospects. But finally, courageously, he agreed to talk. He is sure that Edwards killed Brenda and that Cahoon and the SBI agents blew the case. When some Manteo residents grumbled about Brenda's case being reopened in 2018, Buddy said this: "A 19-year-old girl left this town in a body bag, and they didn't do half of what they should have done to find her killer."

The questions abounded. Agent Cummings seemed to be doing his best at finding answers, including by interviewing Dotty's daughter, Claudia. That took place at 2:00 p.m. on Wednesday, June 13, 2018, at the Dare County Sheriff's Office in Manteo. The office was no longer crammed into the old courthouse in downtown Manteo, as it had been in Brenda's summer. Now the office is in an imposing brick building, part of the sprawling government complex near the new bypass bridge to Manns Harbor. The real estate and tourism business just beginning when Brenda was there had boomed.

The register of deeds office that Dotty ran also moved out of the old courthouse. It is now in the same building as the new courthouse. Claudia, a deputy register of deeds, carries on her mother's work there. The daughter would speak for her mother that day because Dotty's mind was going. She had recently said that Edwards had killed *her* and thrown her off the bridge to the mainland.

Cummings and Claudia sat down across from each other at a small table. She was fifty-eight, blond and hazel-blue-eyed in a navy cardigan, with a navy-and-white-striped dress shirt, white jeans and black wedge sandals. She met Cummings's gaze kindly but unflinching. She carried the blood of the bedrocks of the island power structure. They didn't want to touch this case. She did because a monster from childhood still haunted her. Cummings started the interview. An abbreviated version follows.

> Cummings: *"How old were you when Brenda was killed?"*
> Claudia: *"Seven."*
> Cummings: *"Were you in town?"*
> Claudia: *"I am 99.9-percent sure I was in Carthage, in Moore County, where I would spend the summers with my daddy's family."* She told him that her father, Wayland Hannon Fry Sr., was a decorated WWII hero who died of a heart attack a few months before she was born. *"He had graduated from Wake Forest, had come down here to teach school and was going on to law school before Mama snagged him,"* she said. Cummings asked her about the time she lived with Dr. Edwards.
> Claudia: *"There was always trauma. There was always fear."*
> Cummings: *"From?"*
> Claudia: *"Just Dr. Edwards himself, 'Papa Doc,'"* she said. Sometimes, she said, Edwards would beat her brother with a belt, occasionally for things she did. She would feel guilty, she said. She said she only had one happy memory of Edwards, jumping up in his arms and saying, *"I love you, Papa Doc."* Edwards smiled, she said.
>
> She took refuge, she said, with her maternal grandmother, Cora Mae Basnight.
>
> She remembered being awakened by a strange noise one night, walking into the kitchen, and seeing her mother on a table. *"It looked like to me she was tied up,"* she said. *"I just ran back to my room."*
> Cummings: *"When were you first aware that he was a suspect?"*
> Claudia: *"I remember hearing about it in school, a lot of people were just talking about it. You just kinda knew it, because everybody was talking*

Dotty's daughter, Claudia, with her grandmother Cora Mae Basnight, in Cora Mae's backyard in the early 1970s. Belva Daniels's house, where Belva met with SBI agents, is in the background. *Courtesy Claudia Fry Sluder Harrington.*

about it: 'Oh yeah, he did it.' Mama was talking about it, but that must have been after he killed himself. Because she would never have done that while he was still alive."

Cummings: "You saw a lot of abuse?"

Claudia: "I didn't know until I was an adult that she had been hospitalized three times for his assaults. She would turn to her doctor in Elizabeth City, whom I'm named for, Claude Fletcher Bailey. She didn't know where else to go. He died a couple of years ago when he was in his 90s." Claudia said her mom's best friend remembered going to visit her in the hospital after one of the beatings. Dotty had broken bones, including an arm in a cast, and contusions. Once, Claudia said, her mother was naked when she escaped from Edwards, and got cuts running through the woods filled with briars. She said her mother did not report the incidents. "She would never tell."

Cummings: "Have you ever been told specifics about this [Brenda's] case from anyone?"

Claudia: "Only from Mama. It was just matter of fact. I just grew up hearing it. He thought she [Brenda] was Mama, he grabbed her, he *raped her and threw her body off the bridge. That was what I grew up knowing. Mama loves shock value. She just loves telling people: 'Oh yes, it was Linus.' I guess it just made her feel stronger because she could talk about it. She's a mess. But everything on this, I just knew. Because of his character, what he was capable of. I just knew…It's just one of those things that everybody knew."*

Cummings: *"The whole character of this case could change if we find photographs* [of Brenda's corpse]…*being able to look at those photos."*

Claudia: *"They existed. I have a memory of the photographs. They were on my Aunt Sarah's desk* [in Aycock Brown' office in downtown Manteo.]*"*

Cummings asked Claudia about the rest of her family, including her uncle, Marc Basnight. He was for years the head of the state Senate, and an especially powerful one, more powerful than the governors who served during his time. Basnight, Cora Mae's youngest child, had only a high-school education, but he'd used his brains and Manteo charm to corral the best and brightest of the highly-degreed lawyers in Raleigh to his point of view, bringing millions of dollars to Manteo and the Outer Banks to support tourism. Claudia told Cummings that Basnight was one of her most beloved uncles, one who called her "Claude" and often slowed his SUV to blow her a kiss while riding through their shared neighborhood, Mother Vineyard. Yep, she still lives there, she told Cummings, near the house where she and her mother once lived with Edwards.

Cummings and Claudia returned to the topic of the photos of Brenda's corpse. Claudia remembered going by Aycock Brown's office after school to visit her Aunt Sarah and catching sight of the photos on her desk. Sarah worked for Brown. Claudia said her mother's best friend remembered Brown showing her the photos, while she was with Dotty.

Cummings: *"My next question: Is there anything you didn't say about him* [Edwards] *you wanted to say?"*

Claudia: *"Yes. Living in fear. Him coming around, banging on windows."*

Cummings: *"So fear is the key word here? That's how he kept everything under control?"*

Claudia: *"Yes. Everything had to be perfect."*

Cummings: *"Tell me about their cars."*

Claudia: *"I just remember him driving a light gray sedan, and Mama driving The Wayward Bus, which was custom-painted on the side. It was a van like a painter might drive."* Several hours after Brenda vanished,

Claudia said, her mother and her best friend were riding on the causeway, toward the beach, when they met Edwards driving his car from the opposite direction. It was around mid-morning on Saturday, July 1, 1967. Edwards was slumped over his steering wheel, Dotty's friend told Claudia, and he was either hungover or still drunk. "He'd been up the beach doing God knows what," *Claudia said.* "Driving like a madman. That he was. He could have been at Kentucky Fried Chicken. He loved that, because Mama didn't cook."

Cummings: "Do you know if he had numerous girlfriends?"

Claudia: "[His mistress] *wasn't denying him anything....He was proud of his body.*"

Cummings: "Did he ever do anything to you?"

Claudia: "Not that I was aware of! If he had, I would have told Grandma and she would have knocked his head off."

Cummings and Claudia got back to Brenda. Cummings said, "Maybe it wasn't mistaken identity…"

Claudia: "I don't think he was out cruising for chicks. [His mistress] *was right there. On this island, everybody knows. You can't hide from anything here. Can I show you a picture I have of Mama?*"

She pulled a photo up on her phone to show the investigator the striking resemblance between Dotty and Brenda. In the photo from the mid-1960s, Dotty is smiling, in satin pajamas in front of a Christmas tree with colored lights. It is the Christmas right before or right after the summer that Brenda vanished. Dotty, smiling sweetly at the camera, does indeed look like Brenda, same short blond hair, same softly attractive looks, same long neck.

One theory of the case, pushed by one of Edwards's sons-in-law, holds that Edwards took Brenda's body out in his boat to dump it. Cummings asked Claudia where Edwards kept his boat. Maybe in the driveway, she said.

Cummings: "So your mom was certain that he was responsible for Brenda's death?"

Claudia: "Yes."

Cummings: "What kind of person do you think would have done this?"

Claudia: "To Brenda?"

Cummings: "Yes. Why?"

Claudia: "Maybe it was his sex drive," *she said.* "And he [Edwards] *had a lot of anger. He was sent to military school when he was young and always resented that. His parents were more concerned with socializing than raising him.*"

Cummings asked Claudia for more details about her mother's physical injuries. Hopefully, she said, you can talk to Mama's best friend and she can give you more. That friend knew a lot about the beatings. Once after Edwards beat her mother, Claudia said, Dotty escaped to that friend's house. Edwards followed her there to bring her back home. "Mama sat up pretty and said, 'Well, I must go home,'" Claudia said.

Cummings: "Did he ever sexually assault her?"

Claudia: "I don't know about that…I don't know if she would have denied him."

They talked on. Claudia told Cummings that her mother returned home a few days after the Saturday Brenda vanished. It was the week of the Fourth of July. Dotty probably had a few days off from her job as a secretary at Westvaco. She was reclining in a lounge chair near the driveway, sunbathing. Edwards drove up, shaken to the bone to see her. "He just fell back against the car and said, 'I thought you were dead.' That's the quote I grew up knowing," Claudia said.

Cummings: "Is there anything else you might want to say?"

Claudia talked about her mother and her best friend riding around in the Wayward Bus in the hours before dawn the Saturday Brenda vanished. Her mother stopped briefly at the house where Danny Barber lived, Claudia said. Barber and Brenda weren't back from their date yet. Dotty was friends with Barber's housemates, Earl Mirus and Rodney Brett. She apparently borrowed a beer and left a note for Mirus and Brett.

As Cummings finished the interview, he told Claudia, "Our biggest problem is the lack of physical evidence." That was the blow that Claudia, Kim Holland Thorn, Buddy Tillett and I had been bracing for.

THE SBI HAD BEEN hinting that there might not be any physical evidence left in Brenda's case. The day after Tony's interview with Claudia, the organization acknowledged that this was what happened with Brenda's evidence. It was just gone, SBI officials said. SBI spokeswoman Patty McQuillan told me:

While the SBI makes every effort to solve each homicide case when their assistance is requested by other law enforcement agencies, some cases remain unsolved for various reasons. The SBI has been revisiting some older, unsolved cases to see if potential DNA evidence is present that could be analyzed with today's technology. However, some of these cases may be 30 to 50 years old and most, if not all of the physical evidence has long been destroyed and the case files may have been purged, causing an insurmountable problem and not leaving much for law enforcement to go on with respect to solving cases.

Officials couldn't say whether the Dare County Sheriff's Office or the SBI lab had lost the physical evidence in Brenda's case. But the sheriff's office was almost surely at fault, either during Cahoon's tenure or soon after he retired in 1982, as the SBI lab eventually sent evidence it tested back to local law enforcement agencies. Sometimes local agencies destroyed old evidence because they need the room it was taking up.

Such losses aren't unusual in old cases, but that that doesn't make them any easier to take, especially in Brenda's case, one of the highest profile the state had seen. The day her body was found in the sound, her devastated mother had carefully and painstakingly removed her daughter's hairs from a curler, at the investigators' request. Now those hairs and everything else were lost. The evidence was gone in a case that was already plagued at so many turns by troubling questions. Losing the evidence was either gross negligence or something worse.

And there was more bad news. Agent Cummings might have been able to discern clues from photos of Brenda's corpse. But shots taken by the state trooper in 1967 had come out blank. Local photographer Aycock Brown had also taken photos, as Claudia told Cummings. She had seen those photos. Lucien Morrissette of Elizabeth City told me that he had seen the photos at the home of SBI agent Lenny Wise when Lucien and Lenny's son, as teenagers, had sneaked into Wise's files. Morrissette, just as Claudia, described details from the photos that match Wise's autopsy notes, details civilians would not have known.

Brown's family had given the Outer Banks History Center in Manteo a massive collection of his work. The collection of thousands of photos, from the years soon after World War II through the 1970s, chronicle the Outer Banks' emergence from desolate dunes to one of the nation's most sought-after vacation spots, a transition that his photos, which he pushed nationwide, played a major role in. But nowhere in the collection could I find a photo of Brenda's body. Much of the collection remained uncatalogued. Neither I nor the tiny staff at the history center could find the photos of Brenda in the catalogued part, nor in forays into the uncatalogued part.

The Office of the Virginia State Medical Examiner, which did Brenda's autopsy, would have almost surely taken photos of her body. But that office told the SBI that it had no record of her autopsy.

There are numerous nonfiction books about the Outer Banks, Manteo, Roanoke Island and the lost colony, but few mentions of Brenda, save for an eloquent passage in Bland Simpson's *The Inner Islands*. There's more concern for that colony that vanished more than four hundred years ago than there is for this woman who honored them in a play and vanished more than half a century ago.

In a garden of stone in a mountain valley, cool on a July afternoon in 2018, I knelt at Brenda's grave, absorbing the words carved into cherrystone: "Always thinking of others, she walked in beauty and grace." I could envision her playing with the little children at the adjacent church. I was there in Canton with her little brother, Charles Hoyt Holland, forever broken by Brenda's death. "I have anxiety attacks if I get around people too long," he said. "I'm damaged. I've never gotten over it. I'm over-protective over anything that can't defend itself, especially dogs. I'm a dog person. She was too. I have never read any of the reports on Brenda's killing like Kim has. They try to keep stuff like that from me because they know I don't handle stuff like that well."

He's a big, gentle man who moves slowly. His right leg was crushed in an industrial accident, and he lost vision in his right eye in a stroke. One of his sons died of an opioid overdose in 2012 and is buried in the family plot with Brenda and her parents. Charles Holland, working at the Canton recycling center, lives on with his pain. He drove me around Canton in his beat-up Nissan Pathfinder, two of his smallest dogs happily riding up front with us. He showed me the field where he and Brenda had that long talk on her last Christmas Eve.

By Jennette's Pier in Nags Head, one of the stops on Brenda's last date, I reunited with Buddy Tillett, who'd reopened the case in 1995 as a Dare County deputy. We did a TV interview on that August afternoon in 2018 and talked to Claudia, Dotty's daughter, and Kim, Brenda's baby sister. Kim had brought along the silver necklace Brenda was wearing when she was killed. I held it, feeling a powerful connection to Brenda. She had worn it on her last night just over fifty years ago, a blink in time when you're sitting by the ocean.

Charles Hoyt Holland stands by his sister Brenda's gravestone in July 2018. *Photo by the author.*

From left to right: The author with then-WTKR reporter Rachael Cardin and former Dare County deputy Buddy Tillett in August 2018. *Photo by Kim Holland Thorn.*

We all talked for a few hours about the case. At the end, the women hugged Buddy. Then they hugged each other, sisters bound forever by the summer of 1967. Conversations like that tend to stick with you. I'll end this book with a chapter about my belief on how and why Brenda was killed.

THIS CASE MADE STRAIGHT

Freedom? Hah! Freedom you call it. But wait 'til the tale is ended.

—*Simon Fernandes in* The Lost Colony

ANTEO AT DAYBREAK, SATURDAY, JULY 1, 1967. It had been a hard night. Just before 6:00 a.m., the sun rose above the ocean up the beach, and mists began to lift off the marshes and sound water surrounding the homes and businesses of Manteo.

In the next few hours, Danny Barber groggily rolled over to find his date, Brenda, gone. One of his housemates, Earl Mirus, cranked up his MG for the long holiday ride to see his girlfriend up in New Jersey. Barber's other housemate, Rodney Brett, got in his car for the fifteen-minute ride to the Carolinian Hotel in Nags Head where he worked. Blocks away, in a Black section of Manteo, "California," two other suspects in the case, in separate houses, John Langston Daniels and John Davis Scarborough, were also rousing, hungover. And in Mother Vineyard, the affluent white section of Manteo, David Edward Whaley was sleeping off his drunken daze at the soundfront house where he and his family lived with his grandfather, the local Episcopal priest. One of his neighbors, Dr. Linus Edwards, hungover-ragged on a few hours of sleep, was dragging out of his haze.

Here is my case for what happened on the night before into the predawn hours of Saturday, July 1, based on numerous interviews and my analysis of the SBI file.

FRIDAY, JUNE 30, 1967. Dr. Edwards was raging, once again, at his wife, Dotty. They had it all and they had nothing. They had the soundfront house Edwards was buying from a neighbor. On weekend nights, they'd settle into cocktails. After a while, somewhere down deep in Edwards's big brain, the vodka would stir up his hatred of his mother, whom he once claimed, as a child, he caught in bed with a man who was not his father. He would accuse Dotty of running around or anything else he could think of. He was an admitted blackout drunk, given to beating the hell out of his wife, putting her in the hospital more than once. They'd been married for three years, and his attacks were getting old. At first, they'd go out to eat and party with Dotty's many friends up the beach. She was old-line Manteo and had tried to incorporate Edwards into her scene. But he inevitably blew it. It was okay to get drunk among their set, but not in a mean and boorish way, as Edwards often did.

Late that Friday night, with Dotty's two young children more than two hundred miles away with the family of her first husband, who'd died eight summers before of a heart attack, Edwards and Dotty stared each other down. Dotty would have preferred to be out somewhere, up the beach where the tension between them would have at least been defused by other couples. But Edwards wanted to stay at home alone with Dotty, where he could control her. The ice cubes clinked in their cocktail glasses as Edwards poured in more vodka. They could have looked out their window at the Roanoke Sound and, across it, the twinkling lights of Nags Head and the yellow sand mountain of Jockey's Ridge. Out there near that huge dune across the water, they could have seen traces of the headlights of cars on the bypass. In one of those cars would have been Danny Barber, tooling along in his white Corvair, with Brenda by his side.

Edwards didn't know who was in the cars as his vodka took hold, but he did know to turn on his wife. They started to argue, perhaps about his jealousy over her friendship with her Westvaco co-worker Earl Mirus, a housemate of Danny Barber's. The dentist thought his wife was having an affair with Mirus. Dotty had denied that. Edwards got angrier and angrier at his wife. They yelled at each other. "I'll kill you," he said, advancing on her.

For the first time in their marriage, Dotty said, at least to herself, "No more. No more of your beatings landing me in the hospital. No more covering up, secrets and lies." She fled out of their house and cranked up her van, The Wayward Bus, and took off, stopping nearby to pick up her best friend. The Edwardses' windows were open. Two of their neighbors, Ray and Jean Stoutenburg, heard the fight, the threat and her van and, later, the dentist's car leaving the house.

Dotty and her friend stopped by Barber's house on Burnside Road. Dotty had friends there, Mirus and Rodney Brett, also a housemate. Dotty went in the place by herself, leaving her friend waiting in the van. Barber and Brenda weren't back from their date. Brett wasn't home from work. Mirus was asleep. Dotty grabbed a beer from the refrigerator and wrote Brett and Mirus a note, thanking them for the beer and saying she was going to a party that night at the Hill House, the Roanoke Island cottage rented by members of the *Lost Colony* crew.

Edwards tore out after Dotty in his Ford Fairlane. He stopped at the house of a friend of hers in downtown Manteo, one of the houses Dotty had occasionally fled to in seeking refuge from Edwards. He barged in unannounced, tearing through rooms looking for her until her friend spoke up.

"What the hell are you doing?"

"Looking for her," Edwards replied.

"She not's here. Get the hell out of here!"

Edwards peeked into the children's rooms before he left. Burning with his imagined thoughts of his wife and Mirus making love, Edwards began to circle the roads around Barber's house, looking for Dotty. Brenda, meanwhile, had decided to walk home from there. She'd done it before, after parties at Barber's house, although she'd never been to his bedroom before. In the predawn hours of July 1, she was weakened and vulnerable.

She told Barber, up in his room that Friday night, that a sexual experience with Rob Breeze had soured her outlook on life. Earlier that week, she'd talked with her boss at *The Lost Colony*, Renie Rains, about the man—that she never wanted to go out with him again. "I'm no good," Brenda told Rains. Rains told her that was not true and tried to cheer her up.

Judging by those statements and other evidence, Breeze had raped her. That would account for the bruising and tearing the pathologist noted. In the late 1960s, women were usually hesitant to report what's now called "date rape." It didn't even have a name then.

The assault had, quite understandably, shaken Brenda. She made out with Barber and let him take off her blouse. Then she said, "No more." He fell asleep. She couldn't, or wouldn't, rouse him to drive her home. There was no phone at the house to try to call someone to come get her. She couldn't let herself stay at Barber's house. She was ashamed of putting herself in the situation where Breeze had been able to take advantage of her. She wanted to get home, to be able to face her boss and her landlord proudly. She decided to walk back to the Twiford house, a distance of less than a mile.

It would be a dark walk, but she was a mountain girl. She had steel from her father, the man who could smell rattlesnakes.

She rose from the bed, walked downstairs, slipped quietly out of the house and started walking. As the clock ticked toward 3:00 a.m., John Davis Scarborough, driving toward the home of his friend, John Langston Daniels, drove his station wagon near Barber's house. In another car, David Whaley drove his buddy Dennis Midgett around the area.

Edwards kept circling the roads around Barber's house, searching for Dotty. He drove by Barber's place and then headed back up Burnside Road, toward downtown Manteo. There were no streetlights. The only light was a crescent moon. Fog was rolling in.

About a quarter mile from Barber's house, Edwards's headlights shone on the back of a woman walking toward downtown Manteo. She was tall and slim with a long neck, her blonde hair cut in a bob. To Edwards's vodka-blurred brain and eyes, that was Dotty. He slammed his car's automatic transmission into "park," hopped out and moved on the woman. She picked up her pace. She carried a large handbag with double straps of thin braided rope over her right shoulder. Edwards grabbed her from behind. The woman screamed and dropped the handbag. Edwards, still holding on to the woman tight from behind with his left hand, quickly picked up the handbag with his right hand. He pulled the straps of the pocketbook over her head, then around her neck, and pulled as hard as he could with both hands, wrapping the straps tight all the way around until his hands met at the back of her neck. He was six feet, two inches tall and 195 pounds, mostly muscle. The woman was five feet, seven inches tall and 120 pounds, in good shape but no match for the size and anger of her attacker.

For Edwards, almost half a century of rage against his mother and women in general erupted. The woman struggled against the rope straps cutting into her throat, gasping, trying to elbow the thing that held her, desperately moving her sandaled feet in short but useless steps. Then she was still and dead.

Edwards, drunk as he was, had been surgical in his execution. He slammed her body to the road, hard. She landed on her left side, her face turned away from him in the darkness. Edwards grabbed the shoulder bag off the body and threw it in the front seat of his car. He opened his car trunk, picked up the corpse and threw it in. He climbed in the driver's seat and passed out for a while. Neighborhood dogs started barking. Edwards came to and turned his ignition switch. The car sputtered, coughed and finally started. Robert

Midgett, in his house just up the road from Barber's house, heard the scream and, later, the car sputtering and starting.

Edwards floored it for the Manns Harbor bridge, turning left onto U.S. 64 as Burnside Road ended. After a few miles, he pulled onto the bridge. The hot salt air pouring in through his open window didn't sober him up. At the very top of the bridge, there was a point wide enough to turn a car around. Edwards stopped his car there. From that high point, about midway on the bridge of more than two miles long, he could see the headlights of cars coming from the start of either side of the bridge, from the mainland of Manns Harbor or Roanoke Island. None were.

He opened the trunk. There were no streetlights on the bridge, and there was no functioning light in his trunk. Edwards could hardly see what he was doing. He grabbed the body and threw it over the bridge, throwing out his back or neck in the process. The Croatan Sound was forty-five feet below. Edwards waited until he heard the splash. As he went to close the trunk, he saw that the woman's sandals had fallen off in there. He grabbed the shoes, slammed the trunk and opened his car door, throwing the sandals in. When the interior light came on, Edwards spotted the woman's handbag. He gunned it back for Manteo. As he exited the bridge, he rolled down the passenger's side window and threw the sandals out by the roadside. Then he took a left onto the road leading to the *Lost Colony* theater. He reached in the handbag, pulled out some mascara and a tube of lipstick and threw them out his open car window. He drove a few feet more and pulled a paperback book out of the bag. He was too drunk to make out the title. He tossed out the book. He turned his car around, drove back to U.S. 64 and turned left, headed back toward Manteo.

On Etheridge Road, he turned right and then a quick left onto Scarborough Town Road. That took him through "Up the Road," one of Manteo's two African American sections. Near an asphalt plant, he threw out a purse and more makeup from the handbag and then turned around and, on the other side of the road, threw out the handbag and more makeup. He drove out on Scarborough Town Road toward U.S. 64 and took a left on 64, then drove a few miles to Mother Vineyard Road and turned right. He drove to the end of that road and hung a sharp left to his soundfront house, at the corner of an unmarked dirt road and Mother Vineyard Road. He parked, went in his house and, finding it empty, passed out in the bed he usually shared with Dotty.

He awoke after daybreak that Saturday morning with a pounding head and hazy memories of having killed his wife and throwing her body off a bridge. In the hours ahead, Edwards drove over to Nags Head, for reasons uncertain. As he was returning, Dotty and her best friend, in Dotty's van, were driving over to the beach. At Whalebone Junction, just before the causeway to Manteo, Dotty and her friend spotted Edwards meeting them in his car on the opposite direction of the two-lane road. He didn't recognize them, slumped over the wheel of his Ford Fairlane, either hungover or still drunk from the night before.

Once he got back to Manteo, Edwards invited his mistress over to his house, which he rarely did. His neighbors a few houses over, the Stoutenburgs, noted that her car was there during the day both Saturday and Sunday and that Dotty's van was not there.

Around 1:00 a.m. Sunday morning, Edwards drove to the sheriff's office and reported his wife missing, saying that they'd had an argument a few hours ago and she'd taken off. He asked Deputy Will Daniels to call his mother-in-law's house and ask if any members of the family had seen her. Daniels told Edwards to go home and that they'd call him with an update.

Edwards told SBI agents that he went home, waited about twenty minutes and then went to sleep. Obviously, he wasn't too worried. He reported his wife missing to cover himself because he believed he had killed her. He was lying when he said that Dotty had been home earlier that Saturday night. She didn't return to their home until at least the following Monday—and possibly as late as Wednesday, by Jean Stoutenburg's statement to the SBI. When Dotty did return and Edwards drove up and saw her sunbathing in a lounge chair by their driveway, he got out, fell back against his car and told his wife, "I thought you were dead," Dotty had said.

For a short while, Edwards might have thought his memory of killing a woman the previous Saturday was just some sort of alcoholic hallucination. Then, the Thursday of that week, Brenda's body was found. Edwards realized that he'd killed the wrong woman.

In the days ahead, he wore an upper body cast for either a neck or back injury, the origin of which, apparently, neither Cahoon nor the SBI asked about. Edwards also secured a prescription for 100mg of Demerol, apparently for that injury but maybe also to numb himself for the polygraph test, which he was certainly smart enough to know was coming. He, of course, passed the test. He was a blackout drunk, and he was possibly zonked on Demerol.

EDWARDS WAS AN EXTREMELY intelligent and high-functioning alcoholic. It might seem inconceivable that someone very drunk could have driven to the midpoint of the bridge and dumped Brenda's body and had the sense to dump her personal items along the way and after. But highly practiced drunks, especially smart ones, can do amazing things.

Edwards disposed of Brenda's body using his car, not his boat. He was not a natural waterman in daylight, much less in the darkness before dawn. Navigating Outer Banks sounds and their shallows is tricky enough in daylight. At night, only experienced boaters could handle the waters in those days before computerized controls. Edwards used his car because he was a perfectionist who had to be in control.

Sheriff Cahoon and the SBI agents never pressed Edwards for inconsistencies in his alibi and on contradictions with the statements given separately by his neighbors, the Stoutenburgs. Cahoon and the agents did not push Edwards hard for a confession or for physical evidence that might have tied him to the crime. There is no reference in my copy of the case file of the lawmen ever testing his car for evidence or searching his home, as they did with other suspects.

From start to finish, Cahoon and the SBI agents treated Edwards deferentially, showing him respect they gave no other suspects. Cahoon told the agents in July 1967 that Dotty wouldn't be likely to talk. The agents followed his lead and left her alone. She could have come forward on her own that summer. Cahoon had created a climate in which she felt no pressure to do so. She was probably afraid that, if she did, Edwards would beat her even more severely and maybe even kill her.

So the lawmen ruled Edwards out as a suspect in late September 1967. They eventually ruled out the other suspects as well, except for Danny Barber. But if he had killed Brenda, he would have had to get her body out of the house, from his room upstairs, and into his car that early Saturday morning with his two housemates downstairs in the small house unaware.

If Barber could have thrown Brenda's body over his shoulder or dragged it down the stairs, the commotion would have surely awakened his housemates. Under intense questioning by Cahoon and the SBI, they reported nothing of the sort. One of the housemates, Rodney Brett, lived in a room directly under Barber's upstairs room. Brett had reported the sounds of what he thought was sex going on in Barber's room and, after that, what sounded like someone leaving the house quietly. He said he did not hear a car start. What he heard was likely Brenda leaving the house to walk home.

Even if Barber had been able to slip Brenda's body out of his house, he lacked the knowledge of the local roads and the bridge. Edwards had that knowledge. And Edwards had knowledge period, more than Barber or any of the other suspects, the kind of Mensa smarts that led him, even blind drunk, to strategically scatter Brenda's possessions across the island, throwing off searchers and then investigators—the items cast on the Lost Colony road in a possible attempt to make investigators look at Danny Barber, as well as the ones on the Scarborough Town Road in a possible try at throwing suspicion at Black suspects. If that were the case, both attempts worked, embroiling searchers in hours of vain efforts in both areas when, to paraphrase Cahoon, he would have been better served concentrating sooner elsewhere. After the searches, the sheriff and the SBI looked at several other suspects and, ultimately, only Barber.

Barber had shifted his story, first saying that he had driven Brenda back to her home at the Twiford house after their date. Then, when confronted by Cora Twiford, he admitted that he not done that, that he had taken her to his bedroom and fallen asleep; when he woke, she was gone. Barber probably changed his story out of confusion and fear. Cahoon and the SBI agents then zeroed in on him. Perhaps they were guilty of "tunnel vision," a common affliction among investigators, especially those who have long worked together, feeling so sure early on that they have the killer that they can't objectively look at other suspects. Cahoon and SBI agent Lenny Wise, who basically led the probe for his agency, had long-standing ties, having both come from mainland Dare and having worked cases together for years. And the following November in Chapel Hill, when Barber told SBI agents that he had removed Brenda's blouse, which he'd neglected to tell them before, he cemented his status as the No. 1 suspect.

The blouse remains one of the most perplexing lynchpins in the case. There is no indication in the SBI report or anywhere else, including my interviews, that it was ever found. Perhaps Brenda, in her haste to leave Barber's room and get back to the Twiford house, left the blouse behind. She wore her teddy, basically a one-piece bathing suit, with her skirt over it, and it was a warm night. It's possible that Barber, realizing that the lawmen were wrongly focusing on him, panicked and disposed of the blouse. It's also possible that Edwards tore the blouse off Brenda and disposed of it.

Barber, just as with Brenda, was an outsider. I don't think Sheriff Cahoon and the investigators consciously went for Barber for that reason. David Whaley was an outsider as well, although his grandfather was accepted because of his status as the local Episcopal priest. The Black suspects were locals, but their pigment put them outside the white power structure. Edwards was an outsider, and not a well-liked one, but he had married into an old Manteo family. They did not like him, but they would not have wanted a trial that would have squarely placed the problems between Edwards and Dotty in the public eye. They are a good family but one, at that time, private with their affairs to the outside world.

Cahoon and the SBI agents, at least subconsciously, would have felt that vibe. They did work the case hard at first, but had Brenda been from Manteo and not from a hollow up in the hills, her killing may well have resulted in a murder charge and, possibly, a conviction for Edwards.

There were the bungles on physical evidence in the case, even for 1967. Cahoon allowed Aycock Brown, right after Brenda's body had been ferried in, to remove her necklace, stripping skin away with it. Brown was a good man who meant well, but he was not a lawman, and Cahoon should have stopped him. Instead, Cahoon soon gave that key piece of evidence to Brenda's family, instead of sending it off for forensic testing. The clothes removed from her body were washed before they were sent off to the FBI for testing. Neither Edwards's car nor his house was searched for potential evidence. In the years afterward, all the evidence gathered was lost. The Dare County and SBI lawmen in the late 1960s and early 1970s had no idea of the advances that would be made in DNA testing. Yet Brenda's case was one of the most high profile in the history of North Carolina law enforcement. It should have been second nature for them, and their successors, to preserve the evidence.

The fact that the evidence was not preserved, from the start of the case to its finish, was, at the least, gross negligence. It's telling that after Dr. Edwards killed himself, Cahoon and the SBI basically let the investigation die.

Danny Barber was not the killer, nor were any of the other suspects except for Dr. Linus Matthew Edwards. He strangled Brenda Joyce Holland in Manteo in the predawn hours of July 1, 1967, at the end of one of the best months in her life, and dumped her body in the sound. He got away with murder.

Epilogue

The dream still lives…

—from the opening lines of The Lost Colony

Y ou can lose yourself and find yourself on an island. In the "Summer of Love," Brenda was slipping her moorings for something new. She came so close.

Her slaying left a huge gap from which some of her loved ones have never recovered. Jean Lipham Oates, her best friend from high school, said that she has not had a close friend since Brenda out of fear losing that friend. "I don't want that pain," she said.

On her worst days, the "what ifs" get to Kim Holland Thorn, like what if her sister had never dyed her hair blond that summer? If she had not, there's a good chance Edwards would not have mistaken Brenda for Dotty that night. Then Kim finds comfort in other things, like a 1997 letter from the boy Brenda taught to swim in the summer of 1967. In that August 24 letter to the *Coastland Times*, David Payne wrote that Danny Barber was not the killer and added:

> *I wanted to let Brenda's family know that Brenda has not been forgotten by the many people of Dare County and The Lost Colony that Brenda touched in her few weeks in Dare County in 1967.*

Brenda on the Nags Head beach in the summer of 1967. *Courtesy Kim Holland Thorn.*

I was 13 at the time. Brenda was a wonderful person—fun to be with. She took time to teach me to swim. She always took time with the children from The Lost Colony…

I have never forgotten Brenda. She really touched my life, and, at the time, it was the first close friend that I had lost.

I do wish, and I know, Brenda Joyce Holland can finally rest at peace when the murder file is marked "case closed."

To Brenda's family and friends, I think we should all ask that a monument be placed in Brenda's memory at Waterside Theater in Manteo.

Brenda touched so many lives; let's not forget her.

As Brenda used to say to me, "Hang in there. It will be all right." I would like to pass to Brenda's sister Kim and the rest of Brenda's family Brenda's those words that I still remember.

Payne had become a buyer and seller of collectible items, haunting flea markets for finds and living up U.S. 64 from Manteo, in Columbia. He died several years ago.

In her personal narrative, Kim wrote about Payne's letter, "This is the type of memory I hold to when I remember my sister. She loved people, she loved life and she touched so many people in her short journey."

Brenda's proud legacy lives. She is still out there, crying out for justice.

BIBLIOGRAPHY

In addition to the SBI file on the case, I drew from articles in the *Dare County Times*, the *Coastland Times*, the *News & Observer*, the *Daily Reflector*, the *Charlotte Observer*, the *Virginian-Pilot* and the *Arizona Daily Republic*. The following books and publications were also of immense help.

Bailey, James. *History of the North Carolina State Bureau of Investigation*. Bailey, NC: self-published, 2020.

Bisher, Catherine W. *The "Unpainted Aristocracy": The Beach Cottages of Old Nags Head*. Raleigh: Division of Archives and History, North Carolina Department of Cultural Resources, 1980.

Gray, R. Wayne, and Nancy Beach. *Manteo*. Images of America series. Charleston, SC: Arcadia Publishing, 2020.

Green, Paul. *The Lost Colony: A Symphonic Drama in Two Acts with Music, Pantomime, and Dance. Memorial Edition*. Chapel Hill: University of North Carolina Press, 1946.

————. *The Lost Colony: A Symphonic Drama of American History*. Edited by Laurence G. Avery. Chapel Hill: University of North Carolina Press, 2001.

Kenny, Vincent. *Paul Green*. New York: Twayne Publishers Inc., 1971.

Khoury, Angel Ellis. *Manteo: A Roanoke Island Town*. Virginia Beach, VA: Donning Company/Publishers, 1999.

Lawler, Andrew. *The Secret Token: Myth, Obsession, and the Search for the Lost Colony of Roanoke*. New York: Doubleday, 2018.

The Lost Colony Official Souvenir Program for 1967. Manteo, NC: Roanoke Island Historical Association, 1967.

McAdoo, Carol, and Donald McAdoo. *Reflections of the Outer Banks*. Manteo, NC: Island Publishing House, 1976.

Simpson, Bland. *The Inner Islands: A Carolinian's Sound Country Chronicle*. Chapel Hill: University of North Carolina Press, 2010.

Stick, David. *Aycock Brown's Outer Banks*. Virginia Beach, VA: Donning Company/Publishers, 1976.

———. *Roanoke Island: The Beginnings of English America*. Chapel Hill: University of North Carolina Press, 1983.

Tate, Suzanne. *Memories of Manteo and Roanoke Island, N.C. as Told by Cora Mae Basnight*. Nags Head, NC: Nags Head Art, Publisher, 1988.

Whedbee, Charles Harry. *Legends of the Outer Banks and Tar Heel Tidewater*. Winston-Salem, NC: John F. Blair, Publisher, 1966.

About the Author

John Railey has spent much of his life on the Outer Banks. A graduate of the University of North Carolina–Chapel Hill, he is the former editorial page editor of the *Winston-Salem Journal*, has contributed to the *Coastland Times* of the Banks and many other newspapers and has won numerous national, regional and state awards for his writing and investigative reporting. He is at work on a book about Andy Griffith's special relationship with Roanoke Island that Arcadia Publishing's The History Press plans to publish in the spring of 2022, and he is also the author of the memoir *Rage to Redemption in the Sterilization Age: A Confrontation with American Genocide*.

Visit us at
www.historypress.com